Help!
My Little Girl's Growing Up

Annette Smith

HARVEST HOUSE PUBLISHERS
Eugene, Oregon 97402

Cover design by Terry Dugan and Associates, Minneapolis, MN

Published in association with the literary agency of *Alive Communications, Inc., 7680 Goddard Street, Suite 200, Colorado Springs, CO 80920.*

HELP, MY LITTLE GIRL'S GROWING UP

Published by Harvest House Publishers
Eugene, Oregon 97402

Library of Congress Cataloging-in-Publication Data

Smith, Annette Gail, 1959-
Help, my little girl's growing up / Annette Smith.
p. cm.
ISBN 0-7369-0279-1
1. Teenage girls. 2. Parent and teenager. I. Title.

HQ798 .S568 2001
649'.133—dc21 00-047118

Printed in the United States of America

02 03 04 05 06 07 08 09 10 / RDP-MS / 10 9 8 7 6 5 4 3

For Mom

Acknowledgments

I owe the greatest thanks to my daughter, Rachel. Though she readily admits that many days she would prefer a mother who makes dinner over one who writes books, Rachel has been a wonderful help and encouragement in the crafting of this one. Not only did she tell me what to write about, she also gave me permission to share many private details and stories from her own life. When I expressed some trepidation about writing an advice book for mothers—seeing as how I've made so many mistakes in the raising of her—Rachel told me not to worry. She gave me her word that she wouldn't get pregnant, arrested, or visibly tattooed—at least until I'm done promoting the book!

My husband, Randy, and my son, Russell, deserve thanks for being my best supporters. They somehow always manage to convince me of their genuine interest in my work. (Not a small task when you realize that this time it's a book written *for* women *about* girls.) They continually compliment and encourage me. Without their unfailing belief in my abilities, some days I'd likely quit.

Louie and Marolyn Woodall, my parents, never waver in their belief that I will succeed in this business of words. There are times I find myself sitting in dazed disbelief at the grace and good fortune I've received. Those are the times they don't even act surprised. How can I fail with such love and support?

I express deep gratitude to my gal pals of the Atta Girls support group. The friendship, encouragement, and prayers of this bunch of writers and speakers have helped make this sometimes lonely business of writing books not so lonely anymore. Thank you, Lindsey O'Connor, Susan Duke, Becky Freeman, Cheri Fuller, Rachel St. Johns Gilbert, Jane Jarrell, Rebecca Jordan, Ellie Kay, Fran Sandin, Kali Schnieders, Gracie Malone, and Brenda Waggoner.

My agent, Chip MacGregor, deserves thanks for helping make this project possible, as do the good folks at Harvest House Publishers. I appreciate all the behind-the-scenes work that goes into transforming my creative dreams and ideas into beautiful books that appear on bookstore shelves. The process still amazes me.

To God be the glory.

Contents

1
It's Great to *Have* a Girl!

It's a Girl!

In a tiny, dark room, with my knees obediently flat but my head raised, I lay on my back and stared at the undulating, hologram-like movements visible on the sonogram screen. My husband, his sister, and my mother—holding in her arms our three-year-old son—watched too. The four of them leaned over my bulging belly, transfixed, squinty-eyed; their heads cocked toward the screen at identical angles. They tried in vain to decipher the confusing images; and unconvincingly they feigned recognition and understanding.

Again and again—up and down, around and across my belly—my physician moved the imaging pickup. He seemed pleased by what he saw and proclaimed my unborn child to be healthy. Finally, after long minutes, his magic wand slowed and lingered over what he seemed to deem an important part.

"You want to know your baby's sex?"

My eyes met my husband Randy's. We'd discussed this. "Yes. We do."

"It's a girl."

"A girl? Really! You're sure?" Unexpected tears wet my lashes, ran down the side of my face. Until that moment, I hadn't realized how much it mattered.

A girl! I was having a girl!

Thank you, God!

Our extended family celebrated that afternoon. And the next. And three months later, when Rachel Erin Smith was born—weighing in at eight pounds and two ounces—we celebrated again. Even today, 15 years later, when I remember the day that I learned Rachel was coming, I feel like throwing a party—because having a daughter, welcoming another female into the family, making room for someone *like me,* has brought an unexpected amount of joy to my life.

I suspect that every mom reading this book feels the same way about her own daughter. Aren't we blessed? Sometimes I admit to feeling a bit sorry for those mothers who only have sons. It's probably best, I muse, that they don't realize what wonders they are missing!

My daughter Rachel, now 15, is practically a grown woman. She is smart, pretty, outgoing, and opinionated. The two of us don't always agree, but we learn a lot from each other. And though this growing up business has been far from easy for her *and* for me (it's not a breeze, I'm convinced, for any mother and daughter), I remain certain that mothering a girl—doing all it takes to raise a healthy woman—is one of the most joyful experiences a mother can have.

Lucy's Boys

Married to a handsome young farmer, Lucy wakes every morning to the self-important crowings of a pair of competitive red roosters and to the impatient bawlings of half a dozen hungry baby calves. She falls asleep each night lulled by the unbroken chirpings of a night full of crickets and by the amorous croakings of a multitude of lonely frogs.

An enthusiastic homemaker and an accomplished gardener, Lucy's summertime table showcases plates of garden-grown sliced tomatoes, platters of skillet-fried yellow crookneck squash, and steaming bowls of shelled-on-the-front-porch black-eyed peas. When the chain connected to the light in

Lucy's pantry is pulled, floor-to-ceiling shelves reveal jars—row on row, gemlike—of her home-canned pickles and preserves, jams and jellies.

Every other morning, during her daily mile-long walk to the mailbox, Lucy gathers fistfuls of delicate roadside wildflowers. Once home, she sets aside the stack of bills, sweepstakes announcements, and department store sale flyers to plunge her thirsty botanical plunder into well-scrubbed mason jars filled with the cool, specially collected rainwater she believes wildflowers like best. Once the flowers are arranged to her liking, Lucy places the fresh bouquets around the house, setting them atop her made-by-her-grandma starched lace doilies. She loves the way the flowers scent the air—though her allergy-prone husband, Ben, complains that sometimes they make him sneeze.

Nobody ever accuses Lucy of not keeping herself busy. What with bottle feeding the calves, tending the garden, and her cooking and canning, she has plenty to do. Especially since the birth of twin baby boys, Lucy has her hands full.

Yet in spite of her busyness, Lucy admits she often finds herself quiet and lonely, looking for something interesting to do. Living so far from town, she misses having neighborhood drop-in company. Since she is a long-distance call from most everyone she knows, the telephone seldom rings. Lucy doesn't care much for television—which is a blessing since rural viewing is limited to one snowy channel. Ben and Lucy live in such a remote area that even the plug-in radio on top of the refrigerator picks up more static than music. For amusement, Lucy reads the newspaper and subscribes to the *Reader's Digest*, even taking the company up on many of their buy-three-get-one-free condensed book offers.

Ben, like most farmers, works from sunup to sundown and rushes in at noon only long enough to swallow a hasty lunch. Lucy's husband's enthusiastic agricultural work ethic makes for especially long days during the summer months when daylight seems to last forever. Many times, she's left with only the twins for company eight, ten, sometimes even twelve hours at a stretch.

A few months back, on a particularly quiet and lonely day, a day on which Ben didn't expect to return home until well after dark, Lucy's trip to the mailbox (a trek made these days pushing an ornery, second-hand double stroller) yielded not just bills and flyers, but a twine-tied, brown-paper-bag-wrapped package, sent to her by her elderly Aunt May. It was when Lucy opened the letter attached to the outside of the package that she realized her relative had received some misinformation.

Dear Lucy, Congratulations on the birth of your twin girls...

Lucy set the letter aside and tore open the package. *Sweet of Aunt May to send something...wonder who told her I had girls?* She lifted the lid, folded back layers of tissue paper, and brought out from the box two of the frilliest, most delicate, pastel pink baby dresses she'd ever laid eyes on. Rows of tiny tucks and yards of gathered lace adorned the bodices of the French-seamed frocks. Mother-of-pearl buttons fastened the tiny round collars, and quarter-inch satin ribbon bows, secured with clusters of seed pearls and love knots, adorned each puffy sleeve.

There was more. Under the dresses, Lucy found two sets of scallop-edged socks, two pairs of rosebud-embroidered booties, and two soft-brimmed white organdy and lace bonnets.

"What a shame," Lucy spoke out loud. Hearing their mother's voice, her boys, still happily buckled into their stroller, smiled, cooed, and kicked their bare feet. "Such sweet little outfits. Too bad. Don't guess you two will be wearing these any time soon."

Then a crazy thought occurred to Lucy.

No.

She couldn't.

Wouldn't.

The idea was simply *too* silly.

But then again, why not? She giggled.

What would it hurt?

Who would ever know?

It *would* be fun to see what they looked like...

Impulsively, Lucy laid her two baby boys on the couch, stripped them down to their skin, changed their diapers, and dressed them in the new outfits—the ones lovingly but mistakenly sent by Aunt May. She buttoned the tiny buttons, slipped on the scalloped socks, tied the ribbons of the sweet little bonnets under her boys' double chins. Agreeable, the two babies cooperated as if they were real dolls, just made to be dressed up by a playful little girl.

Once she'd dressed the boys, Lucy stepped back to admire them. How cute they looked! *What if I'd given birth to twin girls instead of boys?* she mused. *Not that I'd trade these precious guys for anything of course...but...*

Whoomf. Her daydreaming was stopped by the unmistakable sound of a pickup truck's door slamming shut in the driveway. *Whoomf* again. She heard a second door slam. Who would that be? Must be someone lost, wanting directions into town. She pushed aside a curtain and peered out to the driveway. When she was alone, Lucy usually didn't open the door to strangers. Ben advised her, for safety's sake, to pretend that no one was home.

Her heart almost stopped. It couldn't be. Not Ben's truck!

But it was. Lucy dropped the curtain. Knew she was trapped.

From her place in the living room, Lucy felt the front door open and shut. She cringed when she heard Ben's boots cross the hall. She wanted to disappear when she detected a second set of footsteps. Her husband wasn't alone.

"Honey, where are you? Remember my friend Tom?" Ben called to her. "The one I'm always telling you about? My roommate from college? Well, I ran into him at the cafe in town. Brought him home with me. Want to show him our two little men. Lucy?"

She glanced wildly around the room. There was no place to hide. No place to stash the boys either.

And then there they were. Ben and Tom, standing beside a scarlet-faced Lucy. The two men looked from one boy to the other, propped as they were on each end of the couch. No one spoke. Tom gazed gape-mouthed at his friend's smiling, kicking, cooing, twin baby boys.

The ones wearing the pink dresses.

And the rosebud booties.

Bonnets. Tied with satin ribbons.

"Lucy?" Ben finally spoke.

"Ben, I...umm...I was just..." Lucy, hot with embarrassment, could find no words.

"Fine-looking boys," Tom finally stammered politely. "Got yourself a couple of healthy boys. Ben, I've really got to be going. Meeting in town, you know. Nice meeting you, ma'am." He was gone.

Lucy never forgot that day. You could say that Ben never *let* her forget it. After the initial shock wore off, he actually came to see the whole situation as pretty funny. Lucy never did come to find the humor in it, but her sons have grown into sturdy boys and seem unaffected by their afternoon spent playing dress-up.

When the boys were five, Lucy gave birth to another child, this time a girl. And though she wouldn't trade her boys for *anything,* when she dresses this child in a ruffled pink dress and satin shoes, when they have tea parties and picnics, play girl games and go on shopping trips, Lucy thinks to herself, *Girls are great!*

They're Not the Same

Who among us would argue with Lucy's feminine enthusiasm? We mothers of girls share a joy that grows as our daughters grow and mature. Those of us who, like Lucy, are blessed with children of both sexes will never be convinced by experts who tell us boys and girls are the same. Equal? Of course. But alike? Not hardly! For from infancy on, these girls of ours are different from their brothers. They behave differently; they feel things differently. They value different things. Their emotions and feelings lie close to the surface. God made them that way.

Luckily, in the times we live in today, girls can easily be encouraged to express themselves freely and challenged to pursue all the dreams they dare. Though not all behaviors are appropriate at all times—good manners and consideration for others are assumed—we moms can orchestrate a myriad of ways in which our daughters' voices and individualities can be expressed.

Encourage Your Daughter to:

1. Dress the way she feels. She may choose a silky dress and sandals today, jeans and a tie-dyed T-shirt tomorrow. Ask her, "What does your outfit say about you today? Does it express the way you feel inside?"

2. Express her emotions. When she feels happy, then laughter, giggles, and silliness are appropriate. Join her! When she feels sad or mad, a daughter needs to be given permission to cry, offered a safe place to scream, provided with a private place to be still and quiet.

3. Play a sport. From volleyball to tennis, soccer to softball, horseshoes to swimming, there is a game or sport for every girl. Even if she isn't competitive or athletic, participation in a team or individual sport provides a great way to let off steam, develop confidence in her body, and forge friendships.

4. Act silly. Don't cringe when she wears a goofy hat to the mall, walks backwards in public, or tells your best friend a pointless joke. This growing-up stuff is often difficult and serious. Being goofy in their own way is a great way for daughters to relax and lighten up.

5. Be loyal to her friends. Moms can model healthy friendships. Our daughters, by watching how we treat our women friends, learn the value and worth of females. Teach her not to gossip or tear down her girlfriends, but to be truthful, supportive, and compassionate.

She Can Be What She Wants to Be

An aptitude test Rachel recently took at school revealed that she should consider becoming a university president, a pig farmer, or a disc jockey. She doesn't think so. Rachel, like many girls, has her own ideas about career options and the future. Here, in her own words, is how my daughter views her future:

"*Some of my friends want to be teachers, some want to work in business. One girl in my class plans to be an eye doctor and another wants to be a chef in a fancy restaurant. When I got that test back, Mom asked me if maybe I'd like to be a nurse like her. 'No way,' I told her, 'I hate blood and stuff.'*

"Right now I'm not sure what I want to be. I'm positive I'll be going to college, and I know I'll be something—probably a children's social worker. I think I'd like working with little kids. One thing I know for sure. When I'm old enough, I want to get married and have some children of my own—three at least, or maybe even four. Most of my friends think I'm crazy. But none of them like kids the way I do. I can't wait to have some of my own."

When I hear Rachel's words, I think *that's* what's so great about daughters. A girl can be anything she wants to be. Being born a female means being blessed with boundless opportunities for growth, exploration, and joy; it's something to celebrate. As mothers of daughters, we have been given the opportunity to nurture, guide, and encourage our girls to be all God meant for them to be. Our every word, action, and expression can give our daughters the message that, indeed, *it's great to be a girl!*

She Can Reach for the Stars

I have on my desk a small framed drawing of a young girl in flight. Her arms are flung upwards, her dress trails gracefully behind her. She is reaching and stretching toward a shimmering star set in a sky of azure blue. Under the drawing are penned these words: *You will, because you can.* When I think about Rachel and her friends, about women and girls I know—when I remember how strong and confident, bold and beautiful they are, how wondrously God has created them—I agree.

We rejoice and delight in you.

—Song of Songs 1:4

Just Us Girls

1. Some evening when only female members of the family will be home, rent a tear-jerking "chick flick" video. Pile pillows on the floor and feast on take-out Chinese vegetables and rice. When the movie's over, blow noses, wipe eyes, and end the evening sniffling and giggling over bowls of Brownie Nut Fudge Ripple ice cream.

2. Invite a friend and her daughter to a high-school or college women's basketball game. Once a season, if a women's professional team plays nearby, splurge on tickets and have even more fun cheering the winning team.

3. If you work outside the home, switch daughters for a day with a mom who stays home full time or one whose job is different from yours. Each girl can experience the life of a woman who is different from her own mother. Meet at the end of the day for salads and pizza.

4. Purchase plain white canvas caps at a craft store. When your daughter has friends over, set out fabric markers, sequins, patches, glue, and glitter and encourage them to decorate their caps to express their individual personalities. Applaud their efforts. Make and model a cap yourself.

2

What's Going On with My Baby?

Who Would Have Thought?

It was my friend Sheri's turn to drive our two 12-year-old sons, Ryan and Russell, to soccer practice. The boys were buckled into the back seat. Sheri sat alone in the front, feigning the deafness and lack of interest we nosy mothers practice to perfection.

"Have you seen that new girl, Julie?" my son Russell asked his friend Ryan. "I think she's cute. I'm going to ask her to go with me."

"Yuck!" exclaimed Ryan. "You don't want to go with her. I heard something really bad about Julie!"

"I don't believe you. She's nice," said Russell, coming to Julie's defense. "What did you hear about her, anyway?"

Ryan lowered his voice, glanced at the back of his mom's unmoving, obviously oblivious head, "I heard she had a period!"

Sheri, struggling not to giggle, glanced in the rearview mirror and watched as every bit of color drained from poor Russell's stricken face.

A period! Who would have thought that a nice girl like that...

Indeed. Who would believe that these little girls of ours would grow up so fast? Overnight it seems we move from ruffled tights and goodnight stories to developing bodies and long-legged good looks. It's a tough transition for moms and daughters. Lots of changes take place, often occurring at a rate way too fast to suit either generation.

If *ever* a daughter needed love, reassurance, and understanding, it's *now*. Overnight, she needs more privacy. All at once, everything embarrasses her. Unexpectedly, she becomes sensitive and afraid.

Suddenly, she is no longer a child.

And whether she knows it, can admit it, or acts like it at all, it is now that she most needs her mom. She needs Mom to explain things, to be positive about feminine body changes, to answer the questions—even the ones she can't ask.

Perfect As She Is

Sarah considers herself to be a semi-liberated, mostly content, stay-at-home mom. She has been known to canvass prospective voters, change the oil in her car, and bake chocolate oatmeal cookies all in the same afternoon. She volunteers at the local battered woman's shelter, and she and her husband co-coach their daughter's soccer team. Sarah loves her daughter very much and has tried to raise 11-year-old Shelly to be self-confident and assertive—to believe that she can achieve any goal she sets for herself.

One sunny Saturday, Sarah's semi-liberated ideas collided head-on with her daughter's achievements and goal-setting. Freckle-faced, knobby-kneed daughter Shelly announced to her mother that her heart's desire was to compete in the Junior Miss Forest Festival Princess beauty pageant.

Sarah squirmed and tried to stammer out words to explain why she didn't think entering the pageant was such a great idea. She rambled on and on about the problems women face when they are valued only for how they look—not for how smart or athletic or musical or artistic they are. She told Shelly, in long and breathless detail, that only a few years ago women couldn't vote or go to college and weren't allowed to participate in sports—about how, not so long ago, women had precious few choices and couldn't even think of becoming doctors or attorneys or astronauts.

But Shelly didn't want to be an attorney. Or an astronaut. Shelly wanted to be a Junior Miss Forest Festival Princess. It sounded like fun. And besides, she wanted to wear a crown.

Her mom lectured. On and on. She didn't believe in beauty contests. Didn't like them. It was obvious that she detested them, in fact. Though she usually discussed her beliefs with Shelly, allowed her daughter to voice her own opinions, this time she just flat out said no. N–O. No daughter of hers was going to compete in the Junior Miss Forest Festival Princess beauty pageant, or any other beauty contest for that matter.

End of discussion.

Shelly, her feelings hurt, and in *total* disagreement with her mom, responded as any self-confident, assertive, goal-directed 11-year-old would. She ran to her room and slammed the door shut.

Nothing more was said about the pageant until two weeks later, when Sarah drove Shelly and her friend Lacy (also burdened with an anti–beauty pageant mother) to the day-long Forest Festival. The girls ate corn dogs and cotton candy, rode all the carnival rides twice, and even took a quick stroll through the smelly livestock exhibit barn.

At mid-afternoon they perched on folding chairs and enviously watched eight of their classmates parade across the flatbed-trailer-turned-outdoor-runway. Within minutes, one of the speechless participants was crowned Junior Miss Forest Festival Princess, and it was all over.

After the pageant, Shelly and Lacy spent the rest of their money in the arts-and-crafts tent. Some elaborate contraptions handmade of wood and bits of hardware attracted their eyes—and the would-be Forest Festival Princesses emerged from the tent well-armed with *potato shooters.* While the newly crowned Junior Miss Forest Festival Princess was having her picture taken for the local paper, Shelly and Lacy were gleefully pelting unsuspecting festival goers with hefty chunks of prime Idaho spuds. Much to the relief of their semi-liberated mothers, neither girl seemed permanently scarred after being deprived of the coveted cardboard crown.

Later that same fall, I hired Shelly to help Rachel and me rake leaves in our yard. She didn't talk much, seemed a bit blue. Rachel noticed it too, and so I gently probed to find out what was bothering our friend.

"What's the matter, Shelly? You don't seem like yourself. Are you feeling sick? Want to stop for a drink of water?"

"Nope. I'm okay." Silence.

In a minute, Rachel stopped working. Leaned on her rake. "Come on, Shelly," she spoke to her two-years-younger friend. "What's going on?"

Finally, after several false starts, after minutes of stalling and studying her feet, Shelly finally just blurted it out: "I hate growing up! I don't like the way I look and I don't like the way I feel. And I hate boys. They're stupid!"

Well.

Rachel and I looked at each other. *Where do we go from here,* I wondered.

I needn't have wondered. Once Shelly got started she told us everything. She hated the fact that her chest was growing.

It hurt when the dodgeball hit her during gym class and some of the boys teased her about wearing a bra. Suddenly she had pimples and she needed deodorant. This growing up stuff was not for her!

After hearing Shelly out, the three of us went back to our raking. I adopted my best "nurse voice" and gently talked to her about puberty, explaining some of the changes that were happening in her body. Rachel added her reassurance. We tried our best to sound matter-of-fact and positive, but Shelly would not be comforted. She insisted that she did not like growing up. Most of all, she wanted her chest to be smaller.

We continued working together, bagging the leaves and speaking of other things. Rachel offhandedly complimented Shelly on her new boots. Shelly proudly told Rachel that she was wearing a size seven these days, one whole size bigger than her mother wore. I commented that possibly her feet were through growing and had probably already reached their full-grown size.

Oh no. All Shelly's friends' feet were at least a size eight. She wanted her feet to grow at least as big as theirs—hopefully even bigger. Rachel and I both struggled not to smile. Our friend Shelly had just told us that she wanted a smaller chest and bigger feet!

A couple of hours later, when we'd finished our work, I paid Shelly ten dollars and both of us gave her a hug. We assured her that we knew she would grow up to be just perfect. Come to think of it, Rachel and I think she already is—perfect, that is!

Funny Business

It happens to every girl, and it will happen to ours. Sometime between the ages of 10 and 15, our baby will take a look at her body and—with astonishment—realize *there's some funny business going on here.* What used to be smooth is now kind of lumpy. Some parts are heavier. She's rounder in some places; in other areas she's begun to curve in. The hair on her head is oilier, and now there's some strange-looking fuzz where before there was none! She may have pimples, and she doesn't even smell the same.

And if your daughter is like most girls, she will—at first, anyway—feel exactly as Shelly did. *She will not like these changes one bit!*

It's helpful to remind a girl that all this stuff didn't *really* happen overnight, to assure her that her body has been growing and developing since she was a baby in our womb. She needs to be told that every woman matures and experiences body changes throughout her entire life. Moms can, gently and with good humor, point out changes in their own bodies—changes such as gray hairs, wrinkles, and certain parts that have moved south! Now is the time to set the stage for a lifetime of healthy body acceptance.

Girls, even quiet ones, harbor lots of questions about themselves. They wonder if their bodies are normal. They may spend many hours secretly worrying that something terrible may be wrong with them. Some girls ask a million questions, but most girls become shy and secretive. To take the mystery and fear out of some of these strange goings-on, girls need information. Lots of it. They need information even if they don't ask for it, and they need to receive it over and over again.

Discussions about puberty, body changes, and such can be awkward for both mom and daughter. Starting with casual explanations about the less anxiety-producing issues like hair and skin, then working down from there, gets things off to a relaxed start.

Below is a sampling of information girls need, a model of how a mom may choose to address the various topics. Use these examples as a place to start. Delete, expand, or add information appropriate for your daughter.

Beginning at the Top

Short, long, curly, or straight, many young girls notice changes in their hair. Most commonly it becomes oily faster. Shampooing more frequently and using a light touch with the conditioner will generally take care of even the toughest attack of the stringies. (Some girls find it easiest to wash their hair every day when they shower.)

Occasionally a girl's straight hair will develop a bit of a wave. Her friend—the one who's always fussed with thin hair—may find that hers thickens up. Each of these changes is normal. And while adapting to them may result in a few "bad hair days," this is a great time to experiment with different styles and to try out a variety of clips, barrettes, scrunchies, and ribbons.

Most girls experience at least *some* not-so-welcome changes in their skin. We're talking about pimples or zits—acne. These pesky pink spots can appear on the face, the chest, even on the shoulders and back. While most girls will get only a few small blemishes, it's not uncommon to have large painful bumps or to break out with lots of them.

Grandma may blame a girl's pimples on eating greasy foods or something like chocolate, peanuts, or ice cream. But most doctors today say that, while a healthy diet is important for healthy skin, eating specific foods (unless a person is allergic) is not likely to cause breakouts.

Washing the face with a mild soap, then gently drying it and applying an anti-acne ointment, cream, or solution from the drugstore will usually take care of minor skin problems. Lots of products are available. Ask the pharmacist to recommend the one he thinks is best. (Be sure daughters know to follow the directions. Sometimes using too much of a product or using it too often can make pimples worse.)

Dermatologists can treat stubborn acne that doesn't respond to over-the-counter products. Not every girl with mild acne needs to see a doctor, but if the pimples are painful, seem to be getting worse instead of better, or are very noticeable and embarrassing, an appointment should be made.

In the Pits

One of the early body changes a girl may notice is a sprout of dark hair under her arms and down below her belly button. Pretty amazing. One day nothing, the next—my goodness! *Where in the world did that come from?* It seems to happen just that suddenly. It's also around this same time that girls usually notice they're perspiring more heavily and that their underarms smell different than they did before. Many girls become extremely conscious about being clean and smelling nice. Girls need assurance that there is nothing wrong with the hair, or with the smell. God put it there!

Girls should know that deodorant, used to stop underarm odor, is best applied once a day, after a bath or shower. It's made to last a whole day. Antiperspirants stop odor *and* actually reduce the amount of sweating. They help keep a girl dry. However, those with sensitive skin may find that they get a rash when they use an antiperspirant. They should use a deodorant instead. Both products work equally well at controlling odor.

The age at which a girl starts to shave is often a source of conflict between mothers and daughters—probably because

Mom knows what a pain it can be to maintain a hair-free state! Understandably, we want our daughters to wait as long as possible before starting the tedious process. However, it can be very embarrassing if a girl isn't allowed to shave when many of her friends are already doing so. Starting to shave at what Mom considers to be a year or two too young isn't going to affect a girl's character or development in any way. Enduring a year or two of teasing and torment about hairy legs and underarms may.

Razors come in lots of shapes and sizes. Deodorants come in lots of brands and scents. Often we moms assume that our daughters want to use the same type of razor and brand of deodorant we prefer. Sometimes girls want to try a product they've seen in a magazine or their friends use and like. This is a good time to let them make a choice.

A Little Bit Lower

About the same time a girl starts needing deodorant, she's introduced to an interesting additional item of underwear—the bra. Along with all the other body changes that are happening, girls should expect to see their breasts growing and developing. Most girls first notice a slight puffiness or a change in color. Their breasts may feel lumpy and are often very tender. It hurts when someone bumps into the chest of a developing girl. When these accidents happen, girls need assurance that even though it hurts, no damage is done. They need to know that breast lumps are normal and are not a sign of cancer in developing breasts. (Of course, a physician should be consulted if ever Mom suspects that there might be a problem.)

Though wearing a bra is uncomfortable at first for a girl, after a bit of time she usually feels more at ease *with* a bra than without. Many girls prefer wearing sport bras at first. They fit snugly and feel almost like a tank top. Other girls like lacy, ultra-feminine bras. The best idea is for a girl to try on several different styles to find the ones that feel the best.

From studying the underwear ads in the Sunday newspaper, many girls would conclude that chests come in only one size—extra large! Girls need to be reminded that this is untrue. Every girl is different and every girl's breasts will develop at their own speed, grow to be their own perfect size, and be perfectly suited to the individual girl's body.

Really the Beginning

Period. The word itself sounds like the end of something. Honestly?

In a way it is. When a girl starts her period (begins to menstruate), her body alerts her and her mom, with an *outside* sign, that some very important *inside* changes have taken place. The beginning of periods means that the girl no longer has the body of a child. Though mentally, emotionally, and spiritually she has much growing up yet to do, physically she now inhabits the body of a developing woman—a body that within a very few short years will be completely mature and all grown up.

Nearly every girl describes feeling almost exactly the same way about her first period. She talks about a mixed up combination of excitement and wonder and fear and dread. Almost every mom shares those feelings. Our daughters, like us, do not know what to expect. Many things about starting their periods worry them as they do us.

Common Questions Girls Have About Periods

Will it hurt?

Will I bleed a whole lot?

Will people be able to tell?

What if I start at school?

Should I tell my friends?

What about letting Dad know?

Most girls begin menstruating (having a period) when they are between the ages of 10 and 16. When a girl nears the end of her teens, her cycles (periods) will come at fairly regular intervals, say every 20 to 35 days. But until then, most girls have very irregular periods. One girl may menstruate for the first time and then not have another period for six months or more. Another girl may have two periods within a couple of weeks of each other, then another one two months later. This is very normal and is nothing to worry about.

The amount of blood lost during each menstruation can range from one to eight tablespoons. Girls should be told that the blood is released very slowly, over two to eight days. It may range in color from light brown to bright red to a very dark maroon. An assortment of feminine products should be available for a girl to look at and choose from. She needs to know they come with sticky adhesive strips that hold them in place. Applying and wearing a pad occasionally—before she ever needs one—will alleviate her anxiety and fears and make it easier to manage when she does have the need.

Some girls think that a period will hurt like a cut on a finger. While the pain and discomfort associated with periods need not be overemphasized or dramatized, girls should be told honestly that they may experience a heavy feeling in their lower backs and tummies or even some cramping—usually on the first or second day of their cycle. Taking a warm bath or resting with a heating pad may help. Ibuprofen is very effective in relieving menstrual discomfort and, when package directions are followed, is safe for young girls. A girl should be encouraged and empowered to discover and employ the comfort measures she finds most effective. She can begin now to be a responsible caretaker of her own body, learning to treat it gently and with respect for the wonderful gift that it is.

Very often daughters do not have the same experiences with their periods that their mothers have. Some girls feel very energetic when they have their periods. Exercise and activities make them feel better. Other girls prefer to be quiet and even choose to go to bed a bit earlier than usual. One girl may be extremely hungry and devour everything in the house, another girl may not feel like eating much at all. Each of these girls is perfectly normal.

Some girls like talking about their bodies and choose to tell all their friends and their grandmas, cousins, and aunts when they begin to menstruate. Other girls feel shy and embarrassed and don't want anyone to know. Each girl should do what feels right to her. She should tell only those people whom she wants to know, and Mom should respect her privacy. No exceptions.

Most girls worry a great deal about starting their periods while at school, at the movies, or perhaps at a friend's house. Talking about the following situation will help her feel confident about taking care of her own needs should that occur.

Tell her that this is how it sometimes happens: A girl discovers she has started when she goes to the bathroom. She will see blood on her underpants, a bit in the toilet, or will see it on the toilet paper. She should keep a pad in a safe place, such as a locker, a purse, or even a special pocket of a backpack. However, if she starts her period and doesn't have a pad, she can ask for one from the nurse or a teacher if she's at school. If she's away from home, she can borrow one from a friend or a friend's mother or older sister. In a pinch, several layers of toilet paper will do until she can get a pad. Periods most often start with a very small amount of blood, generally not enough to soak through clothing. However, girls should to talk to their moms and plan what to do, should they start away from home.

Be truthful about menstruation. Periods aren't particularly pleasant, but neither are they awful. They are, in fact, an *outside* sign that everything *inside* is working as it should. Menstruation need not stop a girl from participating in sports, studying, or having fun with friends and family.

All girls have lots of questions about their menstrual cycles. Since we moms have been having periods for years, we're the best source of information for our daughters. If a mom has questions herself, or feels she needs more information, excellent books are available. A woman's own family doctor or gynecologist is a handy resource, and he or she will likely have informational pamphlets available for patients. We moms rightly want our daughters to come to us so we may answer their questions and help them not be afraid. Even if they're reluctant, our girls need to hear, over and over again, how much we love them, how perfectly they are made, and that they can ask us anything. *Anything.*

A Gift for a Woman

Rachel, with my permission, had her ears pierced before she turned ten. For several years, I allowed her to wear only tiny stud earrings, denying her the hoops and dangles she coveted so greatly.

"You're too young," I explained. "Hoops and dangles aren't appropriate for little girls. When you're a woman you'll have them, but not until then."

And so, on the morning that Rachel's body informed her *and me* that, without a doubt, she was no longer a little girl—a day that, despite my careful explanations and reassurances, brought tears and fears—I presented her with a tiny, gift-wrapped box. She took the package and, at my urging, lifted the lid. Inside, she discovered a pair of delicate, shiny silver hoops. She looked at me with questioning eyes. One of her hands flitted to her ear, fingering the tiny gold stud she was wearing.

"Every *woman* should have a pair of silver hoops," I told her with a smile. "They look great with practically any outfit. Want to wear them today?"

She did.

I praise you because I am fearfully and wonderfully made.
—Psalm 139:14

Woman Stuff

1. On the same day you shop for bras, do something childish and fun. Suggestions: visit the zoo, eat Happy Meals at McDonald's, buy a toy. Let your daughter know that, just because her body is developing, you don't expect her to be *all* grown up just yet.

2. Present her with a "Girl's Goodie Bag" to use when she spends the night away from home. Cruise the trial-size aisle at Wal-Mart. You'll find an amazing assortment of small-size health and beauty products. Pick up items like hand lotion, dental floss, feminine pads, a razor, shampoo, conditioner, toothpaste, and purse packs of tissue. Stash them in a zip-lock bag or in a small makeup bag. Add a tiny tube of lip gloss and mini bottles of nail polish for fun.

3. Tell your daughter about how you and your friends felt when your bodies started to change. Share your own fears and misconceptions about puberty and menstruation. Let her know that her friends may not always have accurate information and that she should check out any wild stories with you.

3
But I'm Not a Baby Anymore!

Lonely Lap

So enthralled was I with my baby daughter Rachel that for months I could hardly bring myself to lay her down in her crib. Though I hid my feelings, I admit to having found it almost unbearable to let anyone else—even her daddy or her grandma—have a turn at holding her. It was a struggle not to snatch her back from them after only a minute or two. I wanted her in my arms *all the time*—while she ate, while she slept, while she cried, and while she cooed. Guided by powerful maternal intuition and by research I'd read about the physical and emotional benefits of touch, I stroked my daughter's little round face, rubbed her tiny feet, gently massaged her shoulders and back. I could scarcely keep my hands off her, and she seemed to thrive, in part—I believe—because of so much skin-to-skin contact.

Not surprisingly, Rachel grew into a warm, affectionate toddler. At three years old, she loved back rubs and kisses, hugs and tickles. When she turned six and went to first grade, she and I continued to sit thigh-to-thigh as we read stories on the couch, and I always got a squeeze when I picked her up from school. Even later, at age eleven, many evenings while we were watching television together, Rachel would nonchalantly drape herself across my lap, ignoring the fact that her now lanky, often skinned-up legs dangled nearly to the floor.

So I was unprepared, shocked, and hurt when Rachel changed—seemingly overnight. Within months of celebrating her twelfth birthday, my snuggly, cuddly, huggy little girl began to shrink from my touch, to pull away when I draped my arm across her shoulders, to stand rigid when I kissed her cheek goodnight. No longer did she want to sit beside me. In fact, it seemed she could scarcely bear to even stand next to me. So unresponsive was she to my normal embraces, so stiff and unyielding, that I found hugging her about as rewarding as I imagine squeezing an ironing board would be.

My logical attempt to "fix" the problem, which was to become more openly affectionate with Rachel, didn't work. She continued to pull away from me, became as skittish as a colt when I tried even to touch her hand. Why was she acting like this? What had I done wrong? Would my daughter and I no longer be close?

Though the change in Rachel's response to me hurt my feelings terribly at the time, I realize today that I had done nothing wrong. And neither had she. In fact, Rachel's behavior—and my own reaction—were completely normal.

Turning Loose, Holding Tight

It is the necessary, though sometimes heartbreaking (for Mom, sometimes for daughter too) task of adolescent girls to pull away from their mothers. It is their job to cease to be adoring children clinging to their mothers' hands and to begin to explore life as the almost-adults they are. (Think about it. How many of *us* share the same kind of closeness with *our* mothers that we did when *we* were girls?) Rachel's physical pulling away from me was simply a dramatic outward example of what was going on inside her. She was beginning to see herself as separate and different from me. Her behavior was both healthy and desirable.

Often, I've observed, the closer a mom and her little girl have been, the more dramatic and painful (at least for Mom) will be this sudden assertion of independence. Learning to gradually let go, to allow Rachel to take small, appropriate steps toward adulthood has by far been the most challenging of all the parenting tasks I've faced. I plead guilty to trying to keep her small just a little while longer.

It's difficult for our girls, too. They desperately want to grow up, sometimes feel they *are* grown up, but at the same time, deep inside, admit to being fearful and unsure. Sometimes they expect us to treat them as adult women, other times they seem to need to be cared for as if they were little children. Sound confusing? It is—both for them and for us! Often they themselves don't know what it is they need.

The path of a daughter who is becoming a woman is one marked by twists and turns and complicated switchbacks. Hence the challenge. Moms are kept guessing. One evening a daughter behaves like a responsible adult, then the next morning displays the characteristics of a dependent little girl. Short of divine revelation, it can be near impossible to discern which one she is at the moment. Is this lovely creature—the one in our kitchen wearing blue eye shadow and a Mickey Mouse sweatshirt—the woman or the child? Does she need nurturing or space today?

When I talk to other moms, we agree that this transition is difficult for most of us. Knowing what's ahead can help.

The Meltdown

Holding the phone in my hand, I breathed what I freely admit was a desperate, pitiful excuse for a prayer: *Please, oh please let her be home, and let her be able to come.*

"Hello."

"Mom?"

"Yes…Annette! How are you?"

"Oh Mom," I stammered. "I'm *so* glad you're home. I've got a problem."

Did I ever. I had messed up. *Again.* Had read my daughter completely wrong.

We were in the midst of preparing for a momentous weekend. In two days, Randy and I would be driving our son Russell to a seven-hours-away university so he could begin his freshman year of college. It was an emotional time for all of us, especially for me. My baby boy was about to leap from the nest!

School had already begun for Rachel, so she wouldn't be making the trip. She'd been behaving in a very independent and mature manner lately, and I had left it up to her to make arrangements to spend two nights with our neighbor down the street. I knew it wouldn't be a problem. My friend Angela and I traded daughters all the time. When she needed to be away, her daughter, Lauren, the same age as Rachel, stayed with us. The casual atmosphere and relaxed schedules of both our homes made it easy for me to give little thought to Rachel's care while we were gone.

Only when I began to pack for the trip, with Rachel sitting on the end of my bed, did I realize something was wrong. Rachel was *not* all right. She was suddenly teary and fearful, feeling neglected and unloved. What had to me been a respectful acknowledgment of her maturity—allowing her to make her own arrangements—had to her felt like parental neglect.

Despite her assertions of independence and her adultlike behavior of late, right now she was a little girl who needed her mother to take care of her needs. I had been insensitive to her feelings, had misread her mood. Again.

Blessedly, Grandma was able at the last minute to come and stay with Rachel while we made the trip to the university. I worried about her while we were gone, even wondered whether I should have stayed at home and let Randy and Russell make the trip without me. When we returned, however, Rachel and her grandma looked as if they'd had a fun weekend.

Quickly as I could, using the ruse of showing her my flowerbeds, I called Mom outside and spoke to her privately about Rachel. Had she cried while we were gone? Had she seemed mopey or upset?

Why no, not at all, my mom assured me. Rachel had been fine all weekend. In fact, Mom said, she could really see that Rachel was maturing, growing up. The three days had been nice for both of them, like an extended slumber party, two friends enjoying each other's company. Of course she had been happy to come, but had I overreacted a wee bit? After all, Rachel seemed *quite together* for a girl her age.

Go figure.

As I think back over that situation, it occurs to me to offer a word of encouragement: This period of profound transitional confusion doesn't last all that long. Generally, by the time a girl reaches her early to mid-teen years, her moods have settled down, and she's better able to communicate what she needs. By then she can actually tell what's going on herself!

However, lest moms think that, once this phase is past, the bumpy part of the parental ride will be over, I find it helpful to remember the wise words of a beloved comedian—the late Gilda Radner. Her endearing character Roseanne Roseannadanna put it like this:

"It's always something!"

She's *so* right.

Knock Before Entering

When girls reach adolescence, many become terribly modest, seemingly overnight. This natural occurrence is yet one more sign of growing independence and maturity. In a sense, girls this age are claiming their bodies as their own for the first time. That's a good thing! We want our daughters to value and care for themselves, to develop healthy physical boundaries.

Modesty should be encouraged, even if a girl's behavior sometimes seems unreasonable. Granted, it *can* be confusing when just last month Mom had to remind her to put on a robe when boy cousins came to spend the night—but today she's locking the bathroom door just to brush her teeth.

When a girl reaches this stage, she's likely to keep her bedroom door closed most of the time. Who knows what she's doing behind that door? Probably lots of trying on clothes. Just expect that if someone accidentally walks in on her when she's changing T-shirts, a daughter this age is likely to screech and duck for cover. It happens.

Everything having to do with the body—anyone's body—is suddenly humiliating. Buying underwear, especially bras, is a mortifying experience. Almost every girl will get embarrassed if she's along when Mom purchases feminine products. Some even try to hide when toilet paper is added to the shopping cart.

This sudden bend toward extreme modesty can seem silly, especially in casual households where running around in one's underwear is considered the norm. It can be inconvenient in small homes where family members vie for time in a single bathroom and in households where sisters share a bedroom. This change in behavior can seem hilariously funny to already developed siblings who think they see no signs that a younger sister has any reason to start being modest.

No matter. Family members should be respectful and resist all impulses to tease her and make light of her behavior. If a daughter displays a desire for increased privacy—either by her words or her actions—she needs it. She should get it. Mom's job is to see to it that she does.

Finding Balance

As a daughter leaves childhood and moves toward the teen years and beyond, deliberate, thoughtful changes need to take place in our parenting approaches. A shift from *control* and *constant supervision*—both appropriate and necessary for parenting a child—to *freedom* and *increasing responsibility*—essential for preparing a young woman for adulthood—needs to occur.

Think about it. Most daughters will, around age 18, leave home to pursue college or work. Once they graduate from high school, many of them will never again live with us under the same roof. The days we've spent parenting hands-on will be over. No longer will we be continually advising and correcting; no longer will we be caring for our daughters' day-to-day needs. They'll be on their own in many ways.

Time is short! We'd best start preparing them now. Think about your own daughter and the age she is today. How many years are left before she leaves home? Seven? Eight? Less? Will she be ready?

In our attempt to ensure that Rachel will be as ready as possible to be on her own, her dad and I employ the following strategy: Each year Rachel is progressively given more freedoms and increased responsibilities. Our goal for our daughter is that by the time she's in her last year at home, she will be, for all practical purposes, on her own. Living in this situation will give her a chance to "practice" being an adult a whole year before she actually has to behave as one. During this year we will be available to catch her when she falls, to clean up the occasional mess she's sure to make, and to fill in any gaps in the life-skill lessons we've attempted to teach.

This parenting plan avoids the abrupt "cutting of the apron strings" that occurs in many families. When a girl is parented as a child right up until her high-school graduation—patrolled and protected, given few choices to make, and not required to live with the consequences of any of them—then is suddenly cut loose from parental control and care, the results are often disastrous. No wonder. How can she be expected to go from being a child one day to an adult the next? The time to begin making the transition is now. Following are a few helpful suggestions. Pick one or two to try. Tailor your choice to your own daughter's age and personality, but keep in mind that one day soon she will be all on her own. It's not too early to start getting her ready.

Ways to Give Her More Freedom

1. Let her choose her bedtime, when she'll take her bath, when she'll do her homework.
2. Buy her a special calendar to keep track of important days and activities. Give her the option of signing up for piano or voice, being a Girl Scout or a nursing home volunteer, taking speech or drama. Let her determine how many extra activities she can manage.
3. Ask her how she wants to spend her birthday. What will give her pleasure? A party? A best friend coming over? A shopping trip with Mom?

4. When planning for school clothes, tell her how much is budgeted. Give her the opportunity to decide what she needs and how much to spend on various items. She may decide on one pair of expensive jeans instead of three pairs that are more reasonably priced. Let her make the choice.
5. Allow her to decide how clean her bedroom will be. Close the door if her housekeeping standards don't meet yours.

Ways to Give Her More Responsibility

1. Purchase an alarm clock for her. Teach her to get up and get ready for school on her own. If she doesn't get ready in time, allow her to miss school, but also allow her to suffer the consequences of doing so.
2. Show her how to do laundry so that when she needs a certain shirt to be clean, she can wash and iron it herself. Have her begin doing an increasing portion of her own laundry as well as her sheets and towels.
3. Discuss meal planning and cooking. Teach her to prepare simple meals so that when the family is on the run, she can prepare nutritious food for herself.
4. Give her a choice as to when she'll do assigned chores, but let her know she may miss a family or individual outing if she hasn't done her jobs.
5. Teach her about over-the-counter medicine and simple first aid, how you decide when a doctor's visit is needed, and how often a person should see a dentist. Have her call and schedule necessary appointments.

It's Not the Same

It has been said that even children close in age, raised in the same family, experience very different upbringings. As I reminisce with my own siblings, I find that statement to be uncannily true. My brothers and I absorbed and reacted to situations differently. Some family memories that carry great pain or joy for me are ones that they can hardly recall, forgotten scenes that contain no emotion for them. For though we grew up in the same house and had the same parents, my brothers and I did not experience life in the same way at all.

So it is with our budding teenagers.

Our daughters won't have the same teenage experiences we did. Some of them will breeze through what were terribly difficult and painful years for us. Others will suffer in ways we can't relate to, simply because we count our teen years among the best of our lives. It's extremely critical that we moms take care not to project onto our daughters our own expectations and attitudes about being a teenager.

You may have been the outgoing high-school cheerleader, broken the hearts of dozens of male admirers, and spent hours on the telephone with girlfriends. Scarcely able to wait until your 11-year-old daughter reaches *her* teen years, you frequently recount tales about the parties you went to, the experiences you enjoyed, the goofy things you did with your friends. Often you voice the expectation that life for your daughter will include the same kind of fun just as soon as she turns 13.

How is your daughter—the one born quiet and shy, even a bit plain, the one who has only one good friend and prefers to spend her time at home with a book—supposed to feel about herself? About what is ahead? She knows already that she will never be a cheerleader and has wisely accepted the fact that she may not have a boyfriend until college. Can you? Are you able to acknowledge her as she is, to understand and celebrate that God made her this way? Can you set aside your expectations in favor of loving her as she is?

I was a preteen nerd. Without a doubt, I was what I hear referred to these days as a "wanna-be." Sure, I had friends—other nerdy kids like me—but so uncomfortable were my adolescent years that I hold to the feeling that life only began when I escaped from the torture chamber of junior high.

My experiences molded me forever into a champion of the underdog. As an adult in social situations, I always relate best to the person who feels left out, the one not dressed quite right, the one who doesn't know how to fit in. I know exactly how to offer encouragement and comfort to those kinds of folks. How odd it is for me then to find myself mothering a girl who is pretty, popular, and self-assured—the kind of clear-skinned girl who would have had little to do with me, *who wouldn't even have known I existed,* had we been together in junior high. I *don't* naturally know how to guide and comfort her. Often I wonder, *How did a mother* like me *end up with a daughter* like her?

Yet in order to love Rachel fully and completely—as the wonderful, unique person she is—I continually strive to let go of the pain I experienced as a preteen. I am readily giving up my expectation that she will be the same as I.

I'm grateful that she is *not* me. May you be grateful in the same way.

Gone Shopping

Just yesterday, Rachel and I embarked on an out-of-town shopping trip with our friends, Debbie and Leigh Ann. Debbie is my peer, the wife of our church's youth minister, and her daughter Leigh Ann is Rachel's good pal. This day we four gals had taken on an important assignment. Our mission: to find Leigh Ann the perfect swirly, twirly, Cinderella-style dress.

You see, in two weeks our friend is scheduled to compete in a by-invitation-only community-wide talent show. In our small town, the annual event is a big deal. It's no wonder Leigh Ann was chosen to perform; she's an amazingly gifted musician. At 16, the girl sings like a teen angel. And though she loves music of all kinds, for this upcoming event she's decided to "sing opera."

And most importantly—to "dress opera."

Hence our quest.

Not just any gown would do. It needed to be long and full—but not too full; sparkly and a bit shiny—but not too shiny; graceful and flowing—but not too flowing! It should make her look sleek and sophisticated—but at least according to mom Debbie, not *too* sophisticated.

So the four of us drove to the mall, unloaded, and descended on Foley's, a department store favored by generations of Southern women. Once inside, a hopeful Leigh Ann barricaded herself in a dressing room, stripped down to her underwear, and proceeded to try on one dress after another.

> Too short. Too long. Too big in the waist. Too tight in the hips.
>
> Too low-cut. (*Definitely* too low-cut, asserted mom Debbie.)
>
> Too blue. Too silver. Too green.
>
> Not green enough.
>
> Too many sequins.
>
> Not even *nearly* sparkly enough.

Despite the store's great selection, after more than an hour we weren't even close to finding one she liked, and I feared our hunt would be in vain. But then, in the last of the bunch, we found it: The Dress. Midnight blue. Satin with a sheer tulle overlay and delicate rhinestone trim. Not too low-cut in the front, but nipped in at the back just enough to perfectly frame Leigh Ann's slender, fair shoulders. Shimmering and sleek, the dress fit perfectly and was even on sale. Since she already owned matching shoes, after making this purchase Leigh Ann would be all set for the talent show.

Just to be sure, Leigh Ann stepped out of the fitting room, still wearing The Dress, strolled and turned, dipped and bowed. The three of us assured her she looked like a princess. Really. When she was finally satisfied, Leigh Ann worked herself out of the dress, hung it back up, and passed it out to us. She happily zipped herself back into her jeans and laced up her boots. Relieved that our mission had been accomplished, Debbie plopped down the plastic.

Now that we'd found what we'd come for—since the pressure of the hunt was over—the four of us were free to relax, browse, and spend the rest of the afternoon just having some fun. First, we paused for a fortifying snack: ice cream for the girls, lemonade for Debbie, and a mocha iced coffee for me. We sat around a food court table, sipping and slurping and discussing what we wanted to do next. Rachel had brought along her fifteenth-birthday money to spend, and Leigh Ann needed a couple of outfits for school. Debbie and I had nothing in mind for ourselves, but still it would be fun to look. We all agreed we'd like to browse for some jeans, shorts, and maybe some tops.

Up until now, the girls had been in amazing agreement with Debbie and me about fashion. No more. For though we'd had little trouble reaching a consensus on Leigh Ann's talent show dress, when it came to picking out casual outfits, neither we moms nor our daughters dared to cross what we found to be the Great Generational Divide.

Debbie and I were delighted at the styles we found. They reminded us of our own teen years: outfits à la 1970. Peasant tops, tie-dyes, and leather platform sandals caught our eyes. Granted, we weren't tempted to buy them for ourselves; most of the items weren't exactly appropriate for women our age, but they would look just darling on our girls.

"I had a blouse just like that. Only mine was blue instead of white."

"Me too! And remember these? I wore jeans like these in the tenth grade."

"Rachel, Leigh Ann," we implored, our arms draped with the retro threads, "don't you want to try these jeans on? This top would look so cute on you."

Oh no. They did not. In fact, if Debbie and I thought a pair of pants looked appealing, well, the girls acted as if they might actually gag. When we exclaimed over a gauzy blouse with embroidery on the sleeves, the two of them rolled their eyes. They wanted no part of the styles we remembered so fondly.

The sad truth? They wanted no part of our teen years.

And you know what? As I gazed around the store, I observed from the presence of the still-full clothing racks, from the abundance of marked-way-down prices, that *most* teen daughters had rejected that season's predicted hot styles. The designers had goofed. Not enough years had passed for those items to have come back around. It appeared to me that the 1970 styles offered by the stores that spring were going to *stay* in the stores. For while I saw lots of mothers looking longingly, very few daughters appeared interested in trying on.

I suppose it shouldn't have come as a surprise. For no matter how good the relationship is, no matter how well they and their moms get along, few daughters this age want to be their moms made over. We are reminded once again that their developmental task during these years is in fact to become their own separate persons, to discover their identities separate from their moms.

Most definitely, they do not care to look like their moms did when they were teens.

And while there is a down side to this fact, on that afternoon I decided to look on the sunny side of the whole thing: If neither Leigh Ann nor Rachel would be caught dead in the new styles, well didn't it stand to reason that Debbie and I were free to at least try them on?

After all, a touch of braid around the bottom of our stretch jeans would be kind of cute, don't you think? I've *always* thought a drawstring neckline was *very* flattering. And, Debbie agreed, platform sandals *do* make you look taller.

It wouldn't hurt a thing, we agreed, to at least try a couple of things on.

"Go on, girls," we told them. "We'll catch up in a minute."

My dove, my perfect one, is unique,
the only daughter of her mother,
the favorite of the one who bore her.
—SONG OF SONGS 6:9

Staying Close, But Not Too Close

1. If your daughter, like Rachel, goes through a time when she is uncomfortable with hugs and kisses, respect her wishes, but nonchalantly offer a foot rub. Peppermint foot cream smells delicious, and a gentle massage provides a nonthreatening way to maintain at least a *bit* of physical contact.

2. When communication is scarce, write a note or a card telling your daughter how much you love her, how proud you are of her. Slip it under her door, or place it, along with her favorite candy, under her pillow.

3. Admire how your daughter looks in the latest trendy teen fashions, but *never* wear them yourself!

4. Expect that she will ask to make use of *your* makeup and jewelry, but that she will balk at the mere suggestion you would like to borrow something of *hers,* even lip gloss or a hair scrunchie, to wear to work. Be content to share sandwiches and sofa space—but *not* her personal items!

4

Two by Two

A Date to Remember

My friend Allison had the best parents. While most moms and dads (including my own) refused to even consider allowing their 13-year-olds to date, Allison's more permissive, easily swayed *("Please, Mom and Dad...please let me go...just this once...Oh thank you, thank you—you're the best!")* parents consented *("Just this once")* to allow her to go out with Robert Burks—a good-looking, much admired, 17-year-old high school senior.

My friends and I could not hide our envy. Robert was *so* cute. He drove a maroon Grand Prix (white interior, stick shift, bucket seats, and eight-track tape deck), played varsity football, and was president of his class. *He* had asked *our friend* Allison out on a date. We could not believe it.

Allison tried to act cool about the whole thing, but we knew she was excited. We couldn't wait to interrogate her. "Where's he taking you?"

"I don't know, riding around or something."

"Whatcha gonna wear?"

"Just jeans or something. Maybe I'll get a new shirt."

"Are you nervous?"

"Not really....Maybe just a little."

Sure. We knew the truth. Our friend Allison was scared to death.

And she was. In fact, Allison was so nervous that she didn't eat a bite the whole day at school before her date with

Robert on Friday night. That evening, putting on makeup, fixing her hair, trying to look older (striving for 14 at least), Allison even felt a little sick—headachy and a tiny bit queasy.

Nerves. She would be fine.

It wasn't until Robert picked her up—20 minutes late—that Allison learned they were double-dating with two other popular seniors, Liz Owens and Rick Tuggle. Allison didn't mind a bit. Truthfully, she felt sort of relieved that it wouldn't be just her and Robert alone all night—and besides, her friends were going to be *so* impressed!

But Allison's elation was not to last. Once in the car, awkward and ignored, our friend realized she was way out of her league. Allison didn't know any of the teens the other three were laughing and joking about, knew nothing about upcoming high-school events, and felt left out when they talked about where they all might end up going to college.

Worst of all, for some unknown reason Robert was acting like he wished he hadn't asked her out at all. He called her "kid" more than once and took stinging jabs at her for being in only the seventh grade. Feeling increasingly nervous and unsure, Allison fiddled with her bracelet, studied her feet. When the four of them stopped to eat, though everyone else ordered burgers and fries, she asked for a small Coke, nothing else.

"What do you mean, you don't want to eat? That's what we're doing here, Allison. Order something," Robert barked.

Embarrassed and eager to please, Allison did as she was told. And when the food came, she took a few nibbles of her burger. Surprisingly, it tasted really good. So she ate some more. After a few more bites, realizing how hungry she really was, Allison dove right in. By the time the four of them left the restaurant, she had managed to finish a whole hamburger, drink all of her Coke, and eat most of her fries. She was feeling a lot better.

And even though Robert was still acting pretty rude, Allison decided she didn't care. He could just be that way. This was her first date and she was going to have a good time no matter what. So she relaxed, hummed with the radio, and talked a little with Liz in the back seat. Things were looking better. She couldn't wait to tell her junior-high friends about her big night.

It wasn't until the four of them had been riding around for about half an hour that Allison stopped feeling so good. Started feeling really bad, as a matter of fact. First came a cramp—low in her belly. Then beads of sweat popped out on her upper lip. Next, waves of nausea—and the terrible realization that something bad was about to happen. Soon.

"Pull over, Robert."

"What do you mean, pull over? What's wrong with you?"

"I said pull over! NOW!" Allison was rolling down the window.

"What the...?"

Barely five feet tall, Allison got up on her knees in the bucket seat and stuck her head out the window—suddenly racked with huge heaves of nausea. Over and over she retched. Hamburger. French fries. Coke. Allison was mortified, but that wasn't the worst of it. Bent double, Allison involuntarily released—each and every time she heaved—the most embarrassing, unladylike digestive sounds possible from her stuck-up-in-the-air blue jean-clad behind.

Allison wanted to die.

Willed the Lord Jesus to come and take her right then.

But when she didn't and He didn't, the news of her mishap was spread all over school by Monday noon. That was to be a long week for our friend Allison.

Somehow, in spite of her pubescent notoriety and the fact that Robert never asked her out again, Allison (whose name I've changed—at her fervent request) managed to grow up to be a poised and polished mother of three girls. But even today, remembering the fiasco of her very first date makes my friend Allison fidget and blush.

A girl isn't likely to forget something like that.

I suppose the moral of Allison's story is that girls should not go out on dates.

Ever.

Just kidding. But don't we mothers wish! For nothing, *nothing* can more easily provoke our anxieties than our baby daughter's sudden interest in deep-voiced, hairy-legged members of the opposite sex.

Some girls at age 10 are already dreaming of getting married, while others, at 14, have given boys little notice or thought. And as each girl is different, so should a mom's response and handling of the topic vary as well. Thankfully, an interest in boys and dating doesn't happen all at once. Most girls will experience a predictable pattern of developing interest.

First Crush

"Luscious Lemon Ice" was my scent of choice. I wore it every day, dotted behind my knees and dabbed on both my wrists. When Darren, my church's dreamy 25-year-old youth director, innocently told me that I smelled good enough to squeeze—well, I confided in no one—but I knew it could mean but one thing: The man was in love with me.

I was 11.

Most girls, just as I did, experience at least one major crush during early adolescence. The object of their affections will likely be someone older, often a much admired authority figure such as a teacher, coach, or youth worker. Sometimes girls will become enamored with a celebrity such as a singer or actor.

Crushes, while amusing to us (and downright hilarious to little brothers), feel like real love relationships to our daughters and should be respected as such. These fleeting infatuations allow very young girls to experience the pleasurable emotions associated with romance without having to deal with awkward expectations or difficult decisions. Most often a girl believes her crush is a secret and mentioning it to her would cause great embarrassment. Even though it's difficult to remain quiet when a girl spends an hour fixing her hair before soccer practice or talks nonstop about a teacher at school, unless a girl's behavior becomes inappropriate, Mom is best off saying nothing (and doing her best to make sure little brother does the same).

All too soon the Age of the Crush will pass.

Going "Out"

"But where," I ask, "do you go?"

Rachel groans and rolls her eyes.

"The water fountain?" I ask innocently. "Maybe the band hall?" She knows I'm teasing; giggling, she begs me to stop.

Junior high, or middle school, is the place where, for many adolescents, real, mutually agreeable boy-girl relationships first form. Depending on the local jargon, daughters may be "going out," "going together," "going steady." All of this "going" generally entails talking to each other at school and on the phone, seeing each other at parties, and sitting together at ball games, after-school activities, and church. Few girls go out on "real dates" at this age.

While it's natural and healthy for boys and girls to be attracted to each other, the idea of having (and keeping) a boyfriend shouldn't take center stage in the life of a girl this age. Moms can help keep adolescent romances in their place by encouraging daughters to stay busy. Girls who are actively involved in athletics, academics, and family and church activities, and those who have close girlfriends, are less likely to place great importance on boys than are girls who are inactive, lonely, and bored.

When a daughter *does* have a boyfriend in junior high—and many do—Mom is wise if she treats news of the relationship in a nonchalant, casual manner. She can show mild interest in what the boy is like, state family guidelines about phone calls, approve or disapprove plans for meetings, and talk frankly about appropriate and inappropriate behavior.

While junior-high relationships present great opportunities for discussions with daughters about dating, love, and marriage, it's easy for a mom to make too much of a romance that will likely be over by next Tuesday. Too many questions, too much interest shown in the relationship, gives the wrong message, lends the relationship more significance than it deserves.

Born to Run

My friend Jennifer was parenting two teenage girls when my Rachel was yet a toddler. Sharing a pot of coffee with me one spring afternoon, she described her daughters' rigorous track practice schedules. Their coach expected them to run what sounded like a lot of miles to me. After all, they were just teenagers.

"That seems like an awful lot of running," I commented. "Do you think it's too much?"

"No way," was her reply. "This time of year, nothing cures a case of spring fever like laps around the track! I *encourage* my girls to run and sweat. Keeps them too tired to *think* about the birds and the bees, much less *do* anything about them. Besides, who knows? They might win a ribbon or a medal, maybe even a trophy."

Real Dates

Every family has individual beliefs and values about dating. Different areas of the country follow specific cultural norms. Rachel has not yet started to date, but my husband Randy and I have come up with some guidelines we plan to follow when she does begin to go out with boys. Some of our rules may be stricter than what other parents feel is appropriate for their daughter. A few from our list may be more lenient than what some parents feel comfortable with. Families should thoughtfully prepare a set of guidelines they feel best suit their values, their daughter's maturity, and the family's needs.

Rachel's Dating Rules

1. No car dates until her sixteenth birthday.
2. No dating anyone more than two school grades ahead of her or three years older than her.
3. No more than one "alone" date per week. (Group dates, parties, and church activities are not counted.)
4. Boyfriends are welcome in our home. They may be invited over to study, to join us for dinner, or to watch a video. However, a boyfriend may come over only one time during a week.

5. Her dad and I must meet any boy she chooses to go out with.
6. We must know where she is going and what time she will be home. If she is going to be late, we expect a phone call.

Real Life

When Rachel was in the second grade, my husband and I decided to open our hearts and our home to foster children. Among the first little ones placed in our arms was Tony, a darling, 23-hour (not days—hours!) old baby boy. He was scheduled to be adopted, but until a suitable home could be found, Tony was ours to spoil and enjoy. What an easy task! At six pounds, two ounces this baby was simply, adorably, *scrumptious*. At first sight of him, all of us fell madly in love; but it was 8-year-old Rachel who claimed him as her own.

Gentle, cautious, and competent (having had years of practice mothering a large family of well-behaved baby dolls), Rachel fed Tony, bathed him, dressed and changed him. She burped him and bounced him, soothed him and sang to him.

And she asked a lot of questions:

"Mama, why isn't baby Tony with *his* mother?"

"Why would a mother *have* a baby if she didn't want to keep him?"

"But how does a mother get a baby if she doesn't have a husband?"

Tough questions. Ones I had not planned on discussing for several more years. But I did answer them. As best I knew how.

I told Rachel about God's perfect plan for families. I explained to her how it took a mom and a dad to make a baby and how God planned for them to be married and to make a home for that baby. We talked about Tony's mom. I shared with her what I knew about the young woman, explained how she had made choices that were not the ones God wanted her to make.

Rachel and I talked about how, when God's plan for families isn't followed, mommies can have babies without husbands, babies they sometimes cannot keep. I stressed to Rachel how much God loved both Tony and his mother and that there was no mistake anyone could make that would change God's love. I told her that good people, like Tony's mother, sometimes make bad choices, and because of those bad choices, their lives often become very difficult.

We talked about how sad Tony's mother must be, how she must miss him; and together we prayed that God would help her feel better.

Daily we hear of situations demonstrating the pain and suffering that occur when God's plan for purity before marriage isn't followed. While being careful not to judge or place blame, we moms can use the circumstances of those around us to point out the consequences of not following God's plan. An unwed, pregnant neighborhood teen, news reports about sexually transmitted diseases, statistics about abortion—all of these can spark natural discussions about sexual purity, the need to make a commitment to premarital virginity, and the powerful, pleasurable role sex plays in a marriage.

To Help Her Remember

Shortly after Rachel turned 13, her dad took her out to her all-time favorite restaurant—Red Lobster Inn. This was a special occasion, her becoming a teenager, he explained, and so the two of them splurged: ordered appetizers, entrées, and even dessert (cheesecake and key lime pie, I've been told).

Once they'd finished the meal, Randy pulled from his pocket a small silver box. "This is for you," he told her, "to help you remember how special you are."

Rachel opened the box and found inside a tiny silver cross, suspended from a delicate chain.

"Rachel," her dad said, "this cross is a sign of my love for you and my commitment to help you live in a way that will please God. You are a wonderful girl and you've done so much so right. But as you become a teenager, there will be times when it may be difficult for you to behave in the way you know best. I want this cross to be a sign to you that God is always there and I am always there too. I will watch over you and guide you. If necessary, I will disagree with you and discipline you. I will love you and protect you. I will do whatever it takes to help you grow up to be the woman God wants you to be. For you are my daughter and I will always be your dad. Remember. Forever."

This morning, when I watched Rachel slip the silver chain over her neck and adjust her collar so that it hung just so, I saw in her face that she does remember. I trust and I pray that she will always.

Don't let anyone look down on you because you are young,
but set an example for the believers in speech,
in life, in love, in faith and in purity.
—1 TIMOTHY 4:12

Where the Boys Are

1. Encourage your daughter to invite groups of friends, both boys and girls, into your home. Have something active for the group to do, such as volleyball and a cookout if the weather is nice, board games and build-your-own pizzas for indoor fun.

2. Arrange time for your daughter to spend alone with her dad. They can go skating, fishing, out to eat. If Dad isn't around, draft Granddad, an uncle, or some other positive male figure to fill in the gap. Spending time with an adult man will help a girl feel confident in handling herself in social situations with boys.

3. When watching a video or TV program together, point out situations where a female character is behaving appropriately. Discuss times when she is displaying honor, strong character, and healthy self-respect. Talk about the consequences of both appropriate and inappropriate behavior.

5

Putting On the Glitz

Church Camp

Young people attending my church's summer youth camp weren't allowed to wear shorts. The rustic, un-air-conditioned facility was located deep in the forest, where most afternoons temperatures crept close to the three-digit mark. So dense were the trees that nary a breeze could be felt, and even on days without rain, humidity levels hovered near 100 percent.

None of that mattered. The flesh might be hot and sweaty, but the spirits were willing. Climate conditions aside, the year was 1970, and in the notch of the Bible Belt where I lived, long pants were considered to be the only appropriate, acceptable choice of recreational attire for modest Christian women. We girls understood why it was so. In a pre-camp planning session, our youth director's pretty young wife explained it to us. She told us all about boys and young men and how we girls could make them have bad thoughts. I recall nodding in grave understanding and feeling a keen spiritual responsibility. The realization that my naked, mosquito-gnawed ten-year-old legs might cause some innocent Christian boy to lust in his heart incited in me a strange and unprecedented—though not unpleasant—feeling of power.

(Even today, I feel a bit funny when I slip on a pair of knee-length cut-offs before taking a walk. "Are you sure these aren't too short?" I query my husband before setting out. I'm still startled when I meet the matronly wife of a church elder in the grocery store and note orange-skin knees visible beneath well-creased walking shorts. To my knowledge, I'm the only church mother who refuses her daughter permission to wear shorts to the Wednesday night summer youth services held at the church building. It just wouldn't seem right.)

In preparation for my very first session of church camp (you had to be ten to go), my mother and I went shopping for the things I would need. We bought insect repellent and a flashlight with extra batteries, socks and new underwear, and a hot pink floppy-brimmed hat. Once home, we sat side by side on my bed, and Mom carefully marked each and every item with my name and address while I checked them off a folded-and-unfolded, almost-read-to-death mimeographed list titled "What To Pack For Camp." When we were done, my suitcase was so full that the two of us had to sit hard on it to get it to latch. Inside it were half a dozen pairs of blue jeans, eight shirts, a raincoat, extra shoes, soap and shampoo, Band-Aids and stationery, and my Bible and a notebook. Having packed everything needed for my six-day stay, I was ready to go—in the nick of time, I suppose. The church bus would depart for camp at 9 A.M. sharp—in exactly one week.

The night before I was to leave, my mother surprised me with one last camp item. Out of a department store shopping bag she pulled a ten-year-old's fashion dream. Did I like it? Like it! I couldn't believe it. My mother, a woman known to value practicality and frugality above almost everything else, had bought for me a long, one-piece, cotton-polyester jumpsuit. Sleeveless, in a navy blue print with a red tie sash, it was the cutest thing I had ever seen. "I thought you might like something a little special to wear on church night," she explained.

My mother was right. The jumpsuit was perfect for church night. But I couldn't possibly wait until then to wear it. I pulled on my new jumpsuit the first morning of camp and received rave reviews from my cabin mates. I proudly wore it to Group Bible, Arts and Crafts, Canteen, and Horseback Riding. Everyone in my group said it was cute, and I think even some of the older girls noticed it. (My guess is that when everyone else in camp is clad in regulation jeans and T-shirts, a chubby ten-year-old in a patriotic-print pantsuit *would* tend to stand out a bit.)

I enjoyed modeling my new jumpsuit so much that I decided to wear it the second day of camp too. Mom had warned me not to change clothes too much, not to run out of clean things too soon, so I was just following her advice. It wasn't really dirty after just one day's wear anyway.

On the third morning of camp, I crawled out of my sleeping bag and pulled on a pair of jeans. I intended to wear them. Really I did. But when I zipped and I snapped, I found the pants were unbelievably hot and heavy compared to the lightweight jumpsuit—and not nearly as cute. Maybe it would be cooler on Wednesday. I would save my jeans until then. Resourcefully, I dug into my dirty clothes sack and pulled out the jumpsuit. After I spit on my finger and rubbed at the spaghetti stains, it looked all right.

That much-anticipated, first-ever week at church camp passed way too quickly. I loved every minute of it. When Saturday rolled around, I couldn't believe camp was over for another whole year. That last morning, before boarding buses to our own Texas hometowns, my new friends and I clung to each other and cried. We exchanged addresses and autographs and planned to somehow, some way, see each other again before next year.

I wasn't ready for the sight of home.

My mother couldn't possibly have been ready for the sight of me.

She'd been warned by experienced camp mothers to expect me to be a bit grimy—not to be surprised if I arrived home needing a good hot bath—but she couldn't possibly have been prepared for my arrival in clothes so dirty they could stand on their own. My mother's controlled response to the ripeness of my apparel remains to this day—in my mind at least—one of her all-time great parental moments.

Only later, when we were together in my room unpacking my things, did she casually question me about how I'd managed to come home with a suitcase full of clean clothes. Had the camp counselors done our laundry for us?

Well, no. They hadn't. It was just that it had been so hot, and the jumpsuit had been so cool and comfortable, and all my friends had liked it so much that…well, I hadn't intended to wear it every single day…it had just ended up that way, I guessed.

"Of course," my mother said.

Doesn't She Look Pretty

Rachel's need to express her own style has often been a struggle for me. I've not always displayed my own mother's restraint and understanding in such matters. I've let my motherly pride get in the way of Rachel's feelings.

Working as a registered nurse has provided me with an adequate income, an interesting career, and steady part-time work. It has been good for me and my family. But nursing does have its drawbacks. At the top of the list is the fact that ill and injured people tend to *still* be ill and injured when weekends and holidays roll around—days when much of the world is free to enjoy family time.

For me, the years when a hospital job required me to work every other Sunday were by far the worst. I hated the thought of my husband and children sitting in a pew together without me. I missed cooking my special Sunday morning pancakes, and I missed coming home to the after-church aroma of Crock-Pot-cooked roast beef. I missed relaxing and reading the Sunday paper, and I missed taking an afternoon nap with my husband.

But I tried to make the best of it for my family. Randy repeatedly told me not to fuss about being gone. The three of them were fine. Really they were. Cereal was okay for breakfast and McDonald's sounded good for lunch. He was perfectly capable of getting Russell and Rachel ready for church. It was not a problem.

But it *was* a problem for *me.* So I purchased frozen waffles and instant oatmeal for their breakfasts, mixed up juice, and even set their table with place mats, napkins, and forks the night before. I prepared sandwich supplies and raw veggies, cookies, and pudding for them to eat for lunch.

And on those Saturday nights before I was to work a Sunday shift, I laid out Russell's and Rachel's church clothes. There wasn't much to the process as far as nine-year-old Russell went. Locating his worn-once-a-week belt was generally the only challenge. Assembling five-year-old Rachel's Sunday morning attire required more thought. A simple sundress and sandals would never do for *my* little princess. No, she needed frilly panties and a slip, the right tights or ruffled socks—coordinated to go with a starched and pressed dress, well-shined shoes, and a big poofy hair bow. I organized it all, and week after week I compelled poor Randy to endure detailed instructions as to how everything went together. ("Remember, the bow goes in the *back*.") One thing was for sure: Even if I, her guilt-ridden working mother, couldn't be there, my little girl would show up for church looking like she'd stepped out of the pages of a storybook.

I would see to it.

One spring morning—it was a Sunday and I was working—Rachel informed her dad that she didn't need his help getting ready for church. She was a big girl and she could do it herself.

"Sure." (I can just picture him answering from behind the morning newspaper.) Fine with him. "If you need any help, let me know."

Not to worry. She didn't. Needing no assistance at all, Rachel, behind her closed bedroom door, ignored the clothes she was supposed to wear in favor of a unique, painstakingly created interpretation of the then-popular layered look. First, she donned purple tights and a black turtleneck. Over that she pulled on a two-sizes-too-small sleeveless knit dress—navy-and-white striped, embellished with primary-colored bows stitched down the bodice. She topped the dress with a heavy pink-and-turquoise wool sweater-vest. White sandals, three of my beaded necklaces, and a careful smudge of pink play lipstick completed her look.

Rachel was ready for church.

Her daddy finished the paper, looked at his watch, and said to get in the car and be sure to buckle up.

It was Easter Sunday.

Across town, my hospital shift ended at three, and I clocked out. Glad work was over, I was eager to be home, ready to see Randy and the children.

At least I thought I was.

I'd barely stepped inside the house when Rachel raced into my arms. She gave me a tight hug and two sticky kisses.

"Hi Mommy! Did you take care of the sick people today? Did you make them all feel better?"

"Rachel!" I pulled away. "What in the world do you have on? What happened to the clothes I laid out for you? You didn't wear the new dress I made for you? Where is your daddy?"

My husband is the calmest, most laid-back man I know, but I'll never forget the flaming daggers he shot at me with his eyes as he spoke through gritted teeth: "Rachel picked out her own clothes today. She waited until you got home to change so you could see her outfit. She looks *very pretty*. DOESN'T SHE."

The man was not posing a question.

"Why…of course she does," I fumbled. But it was too late. Her trembling, suddenly pale little face said it all. No longer prim and proud of the outfit she'd put together, my five-year-old stood before me, embarrassed, self-conscious, and ashamed of how she looked.

Okay. Tell me again. Where does a mother go to resign?

Some Things Don't Matter

Rachel still remembers that day, still recalls how I hurt her feelings. I've told her several times how sorry I am, how out of line I was to say those words. Kindly, my sweet daughter says not to worry, it's no big deal. But I know it was.

Is it any wonder we mothers find it so hard to get this one right? We give birth to this lovely creature—a tiny baby we dress up and fix up till she looks like a little doll. It's such fun! We almost feel like we're playing dolls again. Grandma admires her and little girls ask to hold her and even total strangers stop us to tell us how pretty she is. We put her in dresses and bonnets, booties and bows—and for a few years, she cooperates.

Then overnight, it seems, she learns to talk and to walk and to squirm out of our arms. Out of the blue, she doesn't want to wear dresses or tights anymore. She *likes* her hair down in her eyes like that. Her top does *too* match her shorts. And *no,* she does *not* want to wear the up-until-now favorite matching mother-daughter outfits. In fact, she doesn't want to wear them *ever again!*

She has her own ideas about cute.

Her ideas are *definitely* not the same as ours.

Grandma wonders how we can let her go out looking like that.

We wonder too.

The times are tough. We get a bit touchy. When our daughters look good, we think we look good. But when our girls go out looking frankly awful—ouch! That hurts our motherly pride. Listen up, moms! No matter how hard this is for us, this is our opportunity to give our daughters room to stretch and to grow. They need the freedom to be different from us. As they develop their own physical, outside identities, so will they develop their own emotional and spiritual identities.

What Will She Wear Today?

Choosing what clothes to wear is one of the earliest and easiest ways a girl can express her unique personality. Thankfully, it's also one of the safest. Though moms and daughters rarely agree on what constitutes high style, this is one area where—within only a few broad boundaries—a girl can be free to explore.

Rules that are too specific can get us into trouble, for teen styles vary wildly from one season to the next, as well as from one location to another. Outfits that my Texas girl Rachel loves might be considered unfashionable by a girl living in

California or Maine. And aside from style, clothing considered appropriate for specific occasions varies widely too. For instance, in warm-weather resort areas of the country, shorts are likely to be deemed perfectly acceptable anywhere a girl might go—even church or a nice restaurant. In other, more conservative regions of the country, casual clothes are appropriate only in casual settings.

Lacking specifics that apply to every situation and knowing how rapidly fads change, moms are better off coming up with general guidelines, and the fewer the better! For Rachel, we've decided on two basic rules regarding what she may or may not wear:

1. Clothing must be modest.
2. Clothing must be appropriate for the occasion.

These guidelines have served our family well. Her dad and I together decide what is modest. We leave little room for negotiation. As her body has changed, so has the clothing we consider okay. We realize that standards of modesty evolve over time (remember the Victorians?), yet we also believe that Christians are not to be conformed to the world and that young women should not intentionally dress provocatively.

However, as long as Rachel's clothing is decent, lots of room is left for discussion over what outfits are appropriate for various occasions. Just because we don't like it doesn't mean she can't wear it. If her clothing choice passes the two basic guidelines, she can wear it.

Even if it doesn't match!

I Think She Got the Point

Shortly after her fifth birthday, Rachel and I made a trip to a nearby shopping mall. It being a weekday morning, few other shoppers were out and about. After making a purchase at J.C. Penney, the two of us made our way back along the length of the mall toward Sears, where we'd come in. We'd passed a few shops on our way when a striking young woman came into view. Heading in the opposite direction, she was walking toward us to the other end of the mall. Olive-skinned, hair piled high, nails long and painted, this woman was sporting an *attitude.* Her three-inch spike heels, form-fitting leather pants, black lace bra, and completely see-through blouse displayed her stunningly endowed figure in a way that left little for us to guess.

I held my breath as we met the woman, afraid Rachel might make some comment.

She did voice her opinion all right, but thankfully not until the woman was out of earshot. "Mama," she said as primly as a preacher's wife, "*that* was *not* appropriate."

I struggled not to grin.

Letting Down Your Hair

Rachel has had long hair, short hair, straight hair, wavy hair, bangs and no bangs, layers and no layers. This week we even have blond highlights, painstakingly applied by her friend Lauren in a lengthy, foul-smelling, late-night bathroom beauty session. Rachel asked for permission do it, and for months I said no. Absolutely not. She was too young to be even *thinking* of coloring her hair. She had *plenty* of years ahead for that. But she kept asking. And respectfully, she asked for the reasons why not. Know what? I could come up with no good ones except that I didn't want her to do it. Finally, I admitted to myself that highlights were:

1. Not indecent.

2. Not *really* inappropriate. Half the girls in her class colored their hair.

And so, reluctantly, I gave her the go-ahead. *It's just hair,* I told myself. *If it looks awful, she'll learn a lesson. And it* will *grow back.*

Surprisingly, it turned out lovely—just a bit lighter than her natural color. Not at all as bad as I'd expected. I know, I know. She could have wanted purple, or burgundy, or navy blue. What would I have done then? Honestly, I don't know. No one said this was going to be easy! But I'm convinced that the more we say yes to the things that don't matter—like hair—the easier it is to say no to the things that do.

Come to think of it, I'm considering a few highlights myself. Wonder if Lauren is free Thursday night?

Makeup

Most little girls love to watch their mothers apply makeup. They pretend to blot their lips and they dream of the time when they too can wear mascara and blush. When they sneak into Mommy's bathroom and come out acting all innocent, smeared ear-to-ear with lipstick, they are *sure* they look gorgeous.

When at age 13 girls apply layers of iridescent eye shadow and paint their nails alternately green and purple, they are just as confident of their beauty. Wise is the mom who tempers her tongue, who speaks gently about her daughter's new look or who says nothing at all.

Different areas of the country will have different expectations as to what age a girl must reach before wearing makeup is considered appropriate. But it's Mom who ultimately decides at what age her daughter will be allowed to wear makeup, as well as how much cosmetic creativity is tolerable. With a few denominational exceptions, makeup is considered neither immoral nor immodest—just sometimes unattractive! I've allowed Rachel to experiment freely with cosmetics and have only asked that she tone it down a bit at church. Rarely have I offered suggestions about makeup application. Not surprisingly, to my knowledge she has yet to take my advice!

Permanent Alterations

Rachel has had pierced ears for several years now. She's collected lots of earrings and enjoys coordinating them with her outfits—and she's positive that if one hole in each ear looks good, two or three or more holes would look even better.

I disagree. Foolishly, I try explain with some sort of logic why I think one ear piercing is okay but more are not. I can't. But this lamentable fact doesn't keep me from trying. "Multiple earrings might be perfectly fine for a rock star, but what if you grow up and become a Supreme Court judge?" I challenge her. "You can't expect to sit on the bench with multiple holes in your ears. Think about it. It just wouldn't look right."

"Mom, I'm not going to *be* a Supreme Court judge."

"Nonsense. You can be anything you want to be."

"When I'm 18," she asserts, "I'll get my ears pierced a second time."

"That will be your choice then. It's my choice now."

And it is. For while allowing leeway is appropriate for hairstyles, makeup, and clothes, when it comes to *permanent* changes to a girl's body, moms hold the final say. Earrings and tattoos and other permanent body alterations may not be moral issues, but they involve lasting consequences. Young girls are not mature enough to make decisions that will affect them for the rest of their lives. Fads come and go. While a kitty-cat tattoo might make a daughter the unchallenged envy of her 12-year-old friends, when she's 31 you can imagine that she'll regret it.

What We Really Want

Allowing our daughters as much leeway as possible in the area of personal appearance makes it easier to stand firm on issues in which there is no place for even a bit of compromise. A healthy mothering style is one in which we allow freedom in non-crucial areas of our daughter's lives, such as personal appearance, yet don't hesitate to exert absolute parental control in critical issues such as safety, health, and morality.

For although we worry and fret and fuss over clothes and hair and makeup, what we mothers really want for our daughters is beauty that comes from the inside, loveliness of spirit and heart. It's our gentle guidance that will lead them in that direction.

Don't be concerned about the outward beauty
that depends on jewelry,
or beautiful clothes,
or hair arrangement.
Be beautiful inside, in your hearts,
with the lasting charm
of a gentle and quiet spirit
that is so precious to God.
—1 PETER 3:3,4 (TLB)

Fun and Fashion

1. Plan a special mother-daughter shopping trip. Visit a variety of stores, have lunch at a special spot, get haircuts, and see a funny movie together.

2. When out shopping, encourage your daughter to try on lots of different styles. If certain styles appear unflattering on her, be quick to lay blame on the cut of the garment rather than allow your daughter to conclude something is wrong with her body.

3. Purchase matching pajamas for the two of you (for some reason, mother-daughter nightshirts or pajamas are generally deemed acceptable by even the most prickly of girls), several pretty colors of nail polish, her favorite snacks, and a variety of fashion magazines. Stash them away. On an evening when Dad and brothers are out, surprise her with a "pajama party for two." Paint each other's nails and look at the magazines together. Observe the styles she likes. Why does she like them? Point out why you think some outfits are appropriate and flattering, why some are not.

4. Ask your daughter to help you pick out an outfit for a special occasion. Let her choose which of your shoes go best with a new pair of slacks. Ask her occasionally whether your skirt is too short, whether your hair looks okay in the back, whether she thinks it's too cold for short sleeves. Be ready to follow her advice.

6 Popularity Plus

Some Gals Just Got It!

"The Funny Kids Project" was created by Grace Witwer Householder. Proceeds from her books (www.funnykids.com) go to charities that help children and families. I share the following story from her weekly Internet mailing:

Brooke, age three, was talking about her imaginary friends at a family gathering. "I have lots of them," Brooke said. And she proceeded to name them.

After Brooke had ended her long list, one of the aunts commented, "My, Brooke, you have more pretend friends than I ever had when I was little. I wonder why that is?"

Without a moment's hesitation, Brooke smiled and said, "I suppose it's because I'm more popular!"

Quantity or Quality?

It's true. Having friends, keeping friends, and learning to be a good friend all become more and more important as a girl gets closer to her teen years. Her choice of friends will determine, to a great extent, whether she will hold to the values we've taught her or become rebellious or engage in risky behavior such as drinking, smoking, or using drugs.

That said, moms need to be cautious. If we focus too intently on our daughters' friendships—or on their apparent lack of friends—we can push our girls towards negative peer groups without meaning to. If we unwittingly give them the message that being popular is the most important thing, that having a large group of friends is what we expect of them, then we put pressure on our daughters to have friends at any cost.

Friendships are important. Popularity is not. Your daughter's being true to herself matters. Being accepted by "the crowd" doesn't. Having one or two or three girls she enjoys spending time with is of much greater value than being accepted by the "in" group. Maybe she will be popular, maybe she won't. It doesn't matter. Our daughter's junior-high social standing isn't a reflection of her worth and value, nor is it of ours. We moms must be convinced that this is true if we expect our daughters to believe it. Girls will take their cues from us.

If our daughter is by nature quiet—a bit of a loner, content to have one close friend—she will not be encouraged by our memory-lane tales of what we and our dozens of teen friends did on Friday nights. She'll likely feel that something is wrong with her and suspect we're disappointed in her being the way she is. She *will*, however, benefit from our modeling for her how to be a good friend—kind, considerate, thoughtful, and forgiving.

If, despite our best efforts to teach her that popularity is unimportant, our daughter grieves over her perceived lack of popularity, if she appears to have *no friends,* she needs our help. Orchestrating ways for her to be with others who share the same interests—such as art, nature, music, or animals—can help her develop relationships with girls outside of her school class. However, if you observe that your daughter is constantly ostracized by other girls, if somehow she always seems to say the wrong thing and do the very things that alienate other girls, she needs help. Seek professional intervention from a counselor who is experienced in the care of adolescent girls.

Occasional loneliness is normal. Having *no* friends is not. It is a clear reason for concern and intervention.

FRIENDS OR FAMILY?

While parents and families continue to have the greatest effect on daughters during these growing-up years, the influence of friends becomes much, much stronger. Even if a daughter has been extremely close to Mom up until now, rare is the adolescent girl who names her mother as her best friend. Though Mom may have been a bosom buddy forever, she should expect to be replaced by peers for at least 15 years or so!

Looking good in front of friends, fitting in, wearing the right clothes, and going to the right places become issues of indescribable importance. The telephone becomes as vital in the life of a girl wanting to stay connected to her friends as the umbilical cord was in keeping her connected to her mother before birth.

(Hint: The withdrawal of telephone privileges has been *the most* effective form of discipline in our house. I highly recommend it—along with the installation of a second phone line the minute your daughter turns 11. Worth the cost? You bet. Ask any parent who, stranded with car trouble in the middle of nowhere, has unsuccessfully tried to call home for an hour and a half.)

Missing an outing with friends, even to do something fun with the family, is viewed by a daughter as a crisis of vast proportions. She feels terrible, certain that everyone will be there but her. *What,* we wonder, *is the big deal about missing one Saturday afternoon of skating? There's always next week.* A friend's daughter explained it to me this way: "We're afraid it will be on *that* trip, at *that* party, during *that* church youth gathering, that something crazy or wonderful or awesome will happen. For years everyone will be talking about it but us. We'll be left out because *we weren't there.*"

Court Them

It's easy to feel disconnected when we realize how much our daughters' lives revolve around friends instead of family. But there's much we moms can do to stay in touch. Say yes, every time possible, to a daughter's requests to have friends over. Be welcoming. Strive to have a home that's comfortable for your daughter's friends. Keep a good supply of snacks stashed in the pantry, have extra pillows and sleeping bags handy, have games and appropriate videos ready for play.

Don't try to be in the thick of things when your daughter has friends over; give them some privacy. But don't feel the need to stay in exile in the back bedroom either. Drift in and out. Make casual conversation. Don't try to be a kid. Just be a mom—a nice one!

Show genuine interest in your daughter's closest friends. Call them by name. Remember their birthdays with cards or cakes. (A Twinkie with a candle will make any girl feel special!) Ask about the new puppy they got last week. Keep up with the athletic teams they play on so you can congratulate them on a win. Ask them about last week's family trip out of town. Girls this age love, even *crave* attention from friendly adults. Give it to them.

They'll Never Tell

Tracy and Jennifer met when they were babies and bonded in the playpen. It was bound to happen. When their mothers both ended up in the same Lamaze class—both having recently moved to town, both steely-eyed suspicious of the cheery manner in which "natural childbirth" was presented by their pony-tailed instructor, and both sick beyond words of swollen ankles and stretched-out, ride-up, elastic-waist shorts—a lifelong friendship was begun.

That was 15 years ago. Three more kids, two miscarriages, 33 garage sales, five trips to the emergency room, six part-time jobs, and one divorce later, moms Celia and Jackie remain best friends. They are closer than ever—frequent partners in crime in these their years of almost middle age: in movies, concerts, trips out of town, even a wild, surprisingly profitable home-based business venture. They've never stopped making memories together—don't ever plan to. But it's the early years of their friendship that hold especially good memories for both of them. There's just nothing like those new-mother years, they wistfully agree, nothing like those first babies.

Celia and Jackie take lots of pictures. The growth of their families is chronicled all over their houses, in boxes, drawers, albums, and frames. Of all the photos Celia and Jackie have collected over the years—images of both their own and each other's kids—they count among their favorites a picture taken of Tracy and Jennifer at the J.C. Penney photo studio—the two of them posed together when they were six months old. Displayed in matching ceramic frames on their mothers' bedroom dressers, the photos show the babies wearing identical yellow-checked sunsuits and bonnets. Pink-cheeked and slobbery with seven chins between them, balanced on their bellies like fat little seals, the girls look so much alike they could easily pass for twins.

They acted like twins too. Tracy and Jennifer grew up feeling equally at ease in either of their houses. And once the two families bought homes next door to each other, the girls, by then scrappy six-year-olds, scampered back and forth from house to house, sometimes a dozen times a day.

They charmed, sassed, and begged—they cajoled each other's mom into giving them privileges—they fought with each other's siblings, wore each other's clothes, and foraged for snacks in each other's refrigerators and pantries. So close were the girls that strangers who watched them at play assumed they were sisters.

Neither Celia or Jackie could have loved the other's daughter any more if she'd given birth to her herself. They were as quick to bandage one girl's skinned knee as the other's, as ready to deliver a much-needed bad-manners scolding to either one of them, equally prepared to dry the hurt-feelings tears of both girls.

What they weren't prepared for was the end of their daughters' friendship. Suddenly, Jennifer wanted nothing to do with Tracy. *Nothing.* Curiously enough, Tracy didn't seem to be bothered in the least. The break was overnight. One day everything was fine—the next, they had cut each other off. They quit calling each other, quit coming over to each other's house, quit eating by each other in the school lunchroom, quit sitting next to each other at church. They acted like they didn't even know each other.

Like they had *never* known each other.

Celia and Jackie were beside themselves. Couldn't figure it out. Couldn't stand it. *Had* to know what was going on. Intense interrogations took place in both houses.

"Jennifer, what happened? I know something did. Tell me."

"Tracy! What do you mean nothing's wrong? The two of you are practically not speaking. I want to know what's wrong."

"Did you have a fight?"

"Are you mad at her?"

"Are you going to tell me?"

"Well, are you?"

"Jennifer?"

"Tracy?"

The girls never did tell their mothers. But they told me. Separately. I'll never spill their secret—I've changed their names for this story—but sadly, there were good reasons for the friendship to end. Choices were made, untruths were told, diverging paths taken. It was true—after what had happened, there was little chance they could still be friends, at least at age 14.

If their mothers knew what I know, they would quit asking. They'd leave well enough alone and be thankful for the way it all happened. They would.

Friends Forever?

Many of us, if we think back to our own teen years, can remember something similar happening to us. A friend we were extremely close to suddenly, *overnight,* wasn't a friend anymore. Don't be surprised if this happens to your daughter.

Think twice before getting in the middle.

There is likely more to the story than you want to know.

Adults learn through experience that good people sometimes make terrible mistakes and that even truly evil people are occasionally capable of magnificently kind deeds. We don't give up on our spouses when they disappoint us, our children when they embarrass us, our friends when they do something we don't approve of. We are able to enjoy workplace coffee breaks with a coworker—even though she lives with her boyfriend. We can share garden hints and tools with a next door neighbor—despite the fact that she has a drinking problem. We can take morning walks with a woman who says she's not sure there's a God. We are able to be friends with all kinds of people—even when we don't approve of things they do.

Our daughters often can't make this distinction. If they have been taught that underage drinking is wrong, they will likely drop the girl who's been their best friend since the sixth grade when she confesses to drinking one wine cooler at a party. Should their favorite same-age girl cousin get caught smoking, they may avoid that cousin from then on. If they learn that a girl in the church youth group has let a boy "get to second base," they may scarcely speak to her again.

The break will be swift.

Adolescents hold to rigid standards of conduct and morality. They see most everything in absolutes: black or white, good or bad, right or wrong. And after all, isn't that what we've taught them? Right from wrong?

Sure it is. We're *glad* they've learned those lessons. However, when we see them hold their friends to rigid standards, when they seem to be self-righteously judgmental, we wonder where we went wrong. Did they miss the part about grace and mercy? We *did* tell them about forgiveness. Didn't we?

We did. But at this age, our daughters aren't able to appropriately apply those principles to themselves or to their friends. At this critical stage, they are deciding (in their minds), once and for all, what kinds of kids they're going to be. They are changing from children who are content to do what Mom says—simply because she says it—into independent thinkers who are expected to have greater control over their own behavior. They are formulating important beliefs. While they're in the midst of this task, there is little room for gray, little room for tolerance, little room for seeing both sides of an issue, little room for being friends—even *friendly*—with someone who does something wrong.

Wise is the mom who trusts that her daughter knows what she's doing in her friendships. In a few short years that daughter *will* understand how to choose good friends, how to live up to her own standards, and how to forgive and accept—without condoning—those who don't.

GOOD OLD JOE

When our son Russell was in the seventh grade, we broke some sad news to him. Our family would be moving to a town three hours away where he knew no one. So distraught was our even-tempered son that he lay down on the carpet at our feet, clutching his head and groaning as if our words were causing him physical pain.

"You'll be okay. You will," we told him. "Listen, Russell. It's not like you won't make *new* friends. It won't be so bad."

But for many months it *was* so bad. Settled into our new town, enrolled in his new school, Russell would come home, drop his books, grab a snack, and plop down in front of the television.

He wouldn't want to talk about it. Any of it.

But I would. Every day, out of my mouth would pop the same series of questions.

"Did you make a friend today?"

"No."

"Did you talk to anyone today?"

"Not really."

"Well, did you sit with anyone at lunch?"

"No, Mom. I didn't."

"*You ate your lunch all alone?*" My baby. Had to eat his lunch alone. Is there anything worse for a mother than the picture of her child eating his lunch at school all alone? I wanted to cry, and sometimes I did—though not when anyone was looking.

After a couple of weeks of this routine, Russell's answer to my incessant questions changed. "Yes, Mom," he announced proudly one Friday. "I made a friend today."

"You *did?* Russell, that's wonderful! What's his name?"

"Uh—Joe."

"Joe? He sounds nice."

"I guess he is, but he gets in trouble a lot."

"He does?" My eyes narrowed. "What kind of trouble?"

"All kinds. Nothing really bad. Joe's a good guy."

And so began a new after school routine for Russell and me. Every day he would come home with something new to tell me about Joe.

Joe had seven sisters. *Seven?*

Joe didn't play football. At his last school he'd been on the water polo team. *Water polo? Hadn't Joe last lived in a town in the Appalachian Mountains?*

Joe got in trouble in computer class for sneaking into the lab early and changing all the screen savers into running advertisements for Joe's Dating Service.

Joe dyed his hair blue for a day and wore seven fake earrings in one ear. (Since Joe got queasy just trimming his toenails, real piercings were sadly out of the question.)

So outrageous would be Russell's tales of Joe's playful misbehavior at school, some days I'd nearly fall out of my chair laughing. Russell would laugh too. Best of all, Russell ate lunch with Joe every day. He told me so.

It was only when I called his hand, when I finally insisted that he bring Joe home to meet me, that I learned the shocking truth: *There was no Joe.* My good-natured son, desperate to escape my questions, eager to make *me* feel better, had invented someone to have lunch with, someone he knew I'd like.

I did like Joe. I wasn't ready to give him up.

So I didn't.

For several more weeks, Russell kept me up to date on his friend's latest shameless shenanigans. It wasn't until a few days before Christmas—and by then some *real* friends had crept into our afternoon conversations—that I realized Joe was no longer around. We hadn't spoken of him in a very long time.

And while Russell's flesh-and-blood friends are nice enough, I admit it—sometimes I miss Joe.

Dear friend,
I am praying that all is well with you.
—3 JOHN 1:2 (TLB)

Fun with Friends

1. Host an annual back-to-school slumber party for your daughter and her friends on the last Friday night of summer vacation. Give them brightly colored pencils topped with goofy novelty erasers to use on the first day of school.

2. On the first Saturday *after* school starts, host a back-to-school brunch for friends of your own. No time to cook? Meet at a restaurant or coffee shop instead. Make it a time of fun and relaxation. Before everyone leaves, pause for prayers for students and teachers and for the upcoming school year.

3. Shoot lots of photos of your daughter and her friends. Always request doubles so she can share. Stock up on inexpensive frames. Frames with a cute photo inside make perfect last-minute girlfriend gifts.

4. Plan an overnight getaway for four. Invite a friend and her daughter to join you and your daughter. Go to the city and shop, visit a museum, feast on a fancy lunch out. Or make the country your destination. Stay at an inn, hike or bicycle through the woods, browse at a rural flea market.

7
Got Any Homework?

THE MAGIC OF READING

I confess. We are the family responsible for the neighborhood mailman's aching back. It's because of us that the poor man now keeps a standing weekly appointment with his chiropractor. Sorry—we Smiths are penitent but powerless. Our family is frankly addicted to the printed word. Since we live in the boonies of east Texas, this is a problem. We reside almost an hour from the closest bookstore, in a town where the only place to purchase magazines is the local grocery store. Craving a greater depth of information than that provided by the checkout-stand tabloids, we have no choice but to rely on the United States Postal Service to provide us with our monthly, weekly, and yes, almost daily fix of reading material. Unfortunately, all that printed matter gets heavy. Just ask our mailman.

At last count, we were subscribing to 21 different magazines and newsletters. Want to read it? We've probably got it. The periodicals in our house range from A to almost Z, from mainstream to obscure, from insightful and intelligent to nothing more than fluff. Among the collections delivered regularly to our house are *American Girl, Brio, Christian Woman, Daughters...Sports Illustrated, Time, Virtue,* and *Wineskins.* We also subscribe to *Good Housekeeping, National Geographic,* and *The Christian Communicator,* not to forget *Country Living, Family in Focus, Guideposts,* and *Southern Living*—among others.

Magazines aren't all the family reads. We are members in good standing of the Book-of-the-Month Club, the Quality Paperback Book-of-the-Month Club, Crossings book club, and Better Homes and Gardens Craft Club. In the unlikely event we're unable to fulfill our lust for books through any of those avenues, online shops like Amazon.com provide a virtual printed feast at the fingertips.

What can I say? We need help.

It shouldn't have come as a surprise that in a house full of readers, daughter Rachel would declare that she wanted to learn to read too. Badly. Was this a problem? One wouldn't think so, except for one small detail. At the time of her declaration she was four years old—smart, but no prodigy.

It wasn't fair. Daddy read books. Mommy read books. Even third-grader Russell read books. She wanted to read books too. Forget all this "you'll learn to read when you go to school" stuff. She wanted to read *now*. She *would*. It was decided.

So one night, exuding total confidence and sporting a nose-in-the-air attitude, Rachel, in pink bunny slippers and a yellow flannel nightgown, padded across the living room and gathered half a dozen of her favorite volumes from a bookcase's bottom shelf. "I'm going to go to bed now and I'm going to read before I go to sleep," she announced to the rest of us.

"You are?" I questioned.

"Rachel, you can't read," brother Russell informed her.

"Yes I can. I *want* to, so now I *can*!" she countered.

"Goodnight, Baby. Sweet dreams," I told her.

Down the hall to her room she headed. On went her bedside lamp—"click" closed her bedroom door. A moment of silence followed.

Randy, Russell, and I looked at each other. I shrugged and returned to my own book. Rachel loved to play "pretend."

But she was not pretending. Not this time. Within a couple of minutes, great sorrowful wails began resounding from her room. Going to her immediately, I found my four-year-old sitting up in bed, surrounded by her beloved books, sobbing with disappointment. She flung herself dramatically into my arms. "I thought I could read but I can't. I'll *never* learn to read." I stroked her hair and struggled to keep a straight face. Not an easy feat.

"Very soon you'll go to school and you'll have a pretty teacher and she'll teach you all about reading. I promise. You will learn to read. You're just not quite old enough yet. How about *I* read to you tonight? Then when you get to be a big girl, you can read to me."

Predictably, in less than two years Rachel was reading, just as I'd promised her she would. At age 15, she's an excellent reader. But tonight, as she and her dad sit at the kitchen table and struggle over complex algebra problems, I think, *Too bad she's never had the same craving to learn math!*

Hitting the Books

Though many girls, like Rachel, attend public schools and thrive, a multitude of alternative educational options are now available to families. Secular private schools, Christian schools, and home-schooling provide wonderful opportunities for a daughter's education. Choosing which path to follow is a decision to be made prayerfully by individual families. There is no one plan best for every daughter. However, one thing *is* the same for every girl: The desire to learn is necessary for academic success in *any* setting. That desire—or lack of the same—helps explain in part why Rachel today is a competent reader yet struggles to pass math.

Moms can help develop this desire by modeling a lifetime of learning. Our own commitment to intellectual growth teaches our girls that education is important for women. Our choices of reading materials and our television viewing habits provide our daughters examples of filling one's mind with worthy stuff. Community colleges, located within driving distance of most towns and cities, provide a wide range of low-cost educational opportunities. Budgeting the time to occasionally take advantage of continuing education courses—whether to enhance our computer skills or to learn cake decorating—shows our daughters that learning is important to us. Besides, the courses can be lots of fun!

Girls' interests in school and their attitudes toward learning run the gamut. My friend Kasie has two daughters. Michelle, her oldest, scored "well above average," was deemed almost "gifted" on a recent intelligence test. Her younger daughter, Misti, scored close to the bottom of the range considered to be "average." Guess which girl does better in school? Guess which one makes better grades? Much to the chagrin of their parents—and to the frustration of their teachers—it's not the naturally smart Michelle, but the harder working, less intelligent Misti who excels academically. Michelle barely squeaks by.

Some girls care fiercely about grades—they sign up for advanced placement courses, compete with their classmates, and chew their nails if they make a B. Others just want to pass. They forget to do their homework, never study for tests, and wait until the night before it's due to write a 12-page, footnoted, cross-referenced research paper. How does a mom motivate the underachiever? How does she calm the over-committed one?

It's all about balance. For isn't that what we really want for our girls? We desire that they do their best and that they learn all they can learn while in school, but we want them to also have fun and enjoy being the kids they are.

Overachievers need to be encouraged to simply do their best—whatever that best may be. They need to be helped to understand they will never be perfect; they need to be taught to accept mistakes and failures. They need help lightening up a bit. While it's likely they will—all on their own—sign up for challenging core academic subjects, like advanced math or science, these girls often need encouragement to participate in creative courses like art or drama. They tend toward perfectionism and need their moms to assure them, over and over again, that they are special and loved, not because of anything they do or achieve, but simply because of who they are—precious daughters. A mother's unconditional love models the love God has for all His children.

Perfectionistic girls—who grow up to become perfectionistic women—often spend lifetimes feeling if they could only "get it right," they would be worthy of the Father's love and mercy. A girl's basic overachieving temperament is unlikely to change, but a mother's gentle guidance and continued acceptance can help her excel, not only in school, but also in spirit.

Underachievers also need to be motivated to do their best—their true best. These girls require much greater parental involvement than their overachieving sisters. As young adolescents, they need established study times, and their homework needs to be checked often. Conferences with teachers may be required regularly. Often these laid-back, procrastinating students hold to the naive belief that somehow it (school) will just all work out somehow. And as long as we keep nudging them, it usually does.

However, as these girls get older our involvement needs to decrease. Maturing daughters must begin to take increasing responsibility for themselves. Standing by and watching while our daughter fails a class is extremely difficult for us, but the experience of suffering the natural consequences of her behavior can provide our daughter with a much needed, albeit painful, wake-up call. Even though good grades are what we want for them in the short term, it's a lifelong internal desire for learning that we really wish to foster in them.

Band Girls

When I was in junior high and high school, I belonged to the Mighty Wildcat Marching Band. Though I blew into a silver flute for five years running, I never became very good. My heart just wasn't in it. Sadly, the organization's enthusiastic director labored under the false assumption that I took band because I possessed a love of music, because I hungered to understand its theory, because I had a burning desire to do my part and help the band advance to the state marching contest.

The truth? I just wanted out of P.E. Band was the ticket.

Happily, band was fun, even for an imposter like me. I liked being a part of a group, and it was especially easy to find a comfortable place to belong in an organization inhabited by so many quirky, original, and funny off-the-wall kids.

Here in the Lone Star State, it's an established fact that, no matter what an individual director's higher musical ideals may be, school bands exist to fulfill basically one function: They march and play at football games. The cheering crowd generally measures a band's merit based on one single criterion: How loud can they can play? Is our team's band louder than the other team's band?

Every Friday during fall, my fellow musicians and I loaded our uniforms and our instruments onto long yellow school buses. We traveled, sometimes for hours, to whatever neighboring town our team was scheduled to play. Once there, we unloaded and settled into the stands and waited for halftime—our time to shine. While the games were being played, you would think we band members would watch and yell for our team. Not so—at least not my friends and I. We giggled and gossiped and flirted with the two band boys who we thought were not *too* sissy. We made trips under the stands to retrieve dropped music and mouthpieces, and we trooped two by two to the restroom, feigning mysterious emergencies that weren't. We learned to play the fight song without getting caught chewing gum.

But mostly my friends and I passed the time by making fun of the cheerleaders. We were really nice to them to their faces, of course. Some of them were our friends, our sisters, or our cousins. We only mocked them behind their backs and sassed them under our breaths and sometimes threw popcorn at them when they weren't looking. Covert cheerleader wanna-bes—every one of us—we said they were stuck-up, complained that they thought they were too good for the rest of us. We laughed at how ridiculous they looked in their short skirts and knee socks. (Brazen observations, I now think, seeing as how we band girls were decked out in wool pants and suspenders, cummerbunds and spats, and tall vinyl chin-strapped hats topped with six-inch royal-blue plumes.)

Of course, we didn't even fool each other. We envied the cheerleaders' every move.

I suppose now that I, a former band member and four-year disrespecter of cheerleaders, have been out of high school more than 20 years, it's only fair that I reap the rewards of my obnoxious behavior. Shocking but true, I now have a cheerleader living in my house. Fridays during fall find my Rachel parading up and down the sidelines waving pom-poms and shouting through a giant megaphone She wears a short skirt and tugs at her socks. But, you know what? She's not a bit stuck-up. Rachel doesn't think she's better than anyone else. She looks *cute* in her cheerleader's uniform.

It's a fact. I'm sure of it. Cheerleaders have changed over the years!

Extra Stuff

Band, Choir, Drama, Dance, and Art. Softball, Basketball, Tennis, and Golf. School Newspaper reporting, Yearbook writing, Photography, and Debate. What wonderful choices! Thankfully, a huge range of extracurricular activities is available for girls to choose from today. Moms should enthusiastically encourage their girls to participate, even in activities that don't particularly interest them. Moms need to readily make the commitment to support their daughters in their efforts. These extra activities, though time-consuming and sometimes a bit expensive, give our daughters chances to excel in nonacademic areas. Along with promoting friendship and group cooperation, they give girls the opportunities to develop and explore talents and interests that may stay with them their whole lives.

No matter what extracurricular activities a daughter chooses to take part in, she needs Mom's guidance and support. Whether she verbalizes it or not, she wants Mom to cheer her from the stands, to applaud her concert, to read and compliment her articles, to support her side in the debate. Her participation in extracurricular activities may require Mom to bake cookies for endless bake sales, pick up her uniform from the cleaners, sew costumes, even dish up nachos at Friday night concession stands. It's a fact that with each higher grade our daughter reaches in school, she requires less help with her academics. It's also a fact that with each year of participation in extra activities, the demand on Mom's time increases.

It's worth it!

Girls today have many demands placed upon on them, especially at school. Academic studies must be balanced with extracurricular activities, friendships with family demands, homework with church activities. When everything in their lives seems to be moving too fast—both for them and for us—they need our love and understanding most of all.

The Backpack

I found myself scurrying around the house, trying to make it look presentable. I had no time to really clean since last-minute guests were arriving in less than an hour. A quick pick-up would have to do, so grabbing a plastic trash sack, I flew through the living room. Soda cans, junk mail, yesterday's newspaper—they all went into the trash. I fluffed the sofa pillows, selected fresh place mats for the table, spritzed and wiped the guest bathroom, lit a scented candle.

Three pairs of shoes, an odd dirty sock, and my husband's jacket all needed to be put away. Rachel's backpack was in its usual place, crumpled by the door, where she'd dropped it after school. *I've told her and told her to put it in her room,* I fumed. *I wish she wouldn't just leave it right there.* Too hurried to call Rachel to come get it, I scooped up the shoes, threw the jacket and sock across my arm, and swung the backpack over my shoulder.

Whew! It nearly broke my arm! My 95-pound-daughter's backpack was unbelievably heavy—so heavy that honestly I could barely lift it. What could she possibly be carrying around that would weigh so much? Tossing the shoes and sock and jacket aside, I set the pack down, unzipped it, and looked to see what was inside. In the main section I found half a dozen textbooks, gym shoes, notebooks—and a jacket, a hairbrush, and Chapstick, and her script for a one-act play. A side pocket held her uneaten lunch. (Because of a school-time orthodontist appointment earlier in the day, I knew she'd had a noontime make-up for an English test today. Had taking the test left no time to eat?) Next to her lunch were crammed her cheerleading socks, a bottle of Midol, a tiny New Testament, and two dog-eared folders labeled "Spanish" and "Speech." Yet another pocket held three dollars in quarters, a handful of pencils and pens, and a picture of her very best friend. Not disturbing or rearranging any of the items, I slowly zipped the backpack back up, then carefully, *prayerfully,* lifted it in my arms.

This is my daughter's life, I thought. *She carries it every day. No wonder she drops it at the door. I never realized how heavy it was!*

That random pause in my housecleaning frenzy took place a few years ago. It changed me in an unexpected way. For after lifting my daughter's backpack, I came to comprehend why she sometimes came home tired, and cranky, and even rude. I still corrected her, and I still tried to soothe her, but after that time I believe I understood better why she sometimes acted so irritable and overwhelmed.

She was.

Lately, I find myself impatient with Rachel, wondering why she doesn't just get her act together. What is wrong with her?

Suddenly I realize—it's been way too long. And so tonight after she's asleep, I'll slip into my daughter's bedroom. Quietly, I'll grope around in the dark until I find her backpack. It won't be hard; I've done this many times before. I'll grasp the pack by the straps, and deliberately, I'll swing it upward till it rests heavily on my shoulders.

I'll hold it there for a moment, feeling its weight, noting the pressure it puts on my back. After a short while, I'll set it back down, then I'll cross the room and watch my daughter while she sleeps.

And once again, at least for a short while, I'll think that I understand.

He gives strength to the weary and increases the power of the weak.
Even youths grow tired and weary,
and young men stumble and fall;
but those who hope in the LORD will renew their strength.
They will soar on wings like eagles;
they will run and not grow weary,
they will walk and not be faint.

—ISAIAH 40:29-31

Learning Is a Good Thing!

1. If your family lives near a college or university, befriend a female student. Invite her to share meals, do laundry, relax on Sunday afternoons. Developing a relationship with the student will give your daughter someone to admire and emulate.

2. Look for continuing-education classes you and your daughter can attend together. Discover a new craft, study conversational French, learn to develop photographs.

3. As soon as your daughter is old enough, share books. Rachel and I both recently read *To Kill a Mockingbird* and *The Hiding Place.* It was fun and stimulating for us to share ideas about the characters, their motivations, and the consequences of their actions.

8
I've Already Spent My Allowance—and It's Only Tuesday!

Everything's Coming Up Green

When Rachel was four years old, her favorite way to spend a morning was to tag along with me while I was running errands. Though I didn't particularly enjoy what I considered a mindless, time-consuming task, she loved every minute of it. The more stops we had on our list, the better she liked it.

And so, every Tuesday right after breakfast, the two of us would tidy up, wash up, load up, and buckle up, and set out on our rounds. First we'd swing by the bank and the post office. Then we'd stop by the dry cleaner's, cruise through Wal-Mart, and zip into the pharmacy. At each place of business, Rachel would carefully observe the staff as they carried out their jobs. Not one task they performed escaped her intense observation. She enjoyed the outing so much that rarely did she get tired, complain, or ask to go home.

We always saved the grocery store till last. Often I'd treat the two of us to a cookie or a scoop of ice cream on the way home. Sometimes, if I'd planned ahead, we would meet another mother and daughter for lunch. Rachel's favorite restaurant was the Chinese place, where she routinely ordered steamed white rice topped with sweet-and-sour sauce, along with a cherry Coke to drink.

Once we arrived back at home, after putting our purchases away I'd usually make myself a cup of tea and put my feet up. I'd allow myself a half-hour break to read a chapter or two of a novel or to watch some television before getting on with the day's tasks. Running errands tired me out!

Not Rachel. This little girl had lots to do. Every Tuesday, as soon as we were inside the house, she was hard at work setting up a pretend place of business. Some days Rachel played "pharmacy," taking refill orders over her toy telephone and making detailed notes (in script only *she* could "read"). Using buttons and empty baby food jars, she carefully filled much needed prescriptions for imaginary mothers of very sick baby dolls. As head pharmacist, she sternly gave detailed instructions to each and every customer.

"Give her 17 pills when she gets up from her nap."

"Call the doctor if he doesn't stop coughing by snack time."

"These pills will make him cry, but he has to take them anyway."

Pharmacy wasn't Rachel's only entrepreneurial venture. Some Tuesdays, the day's toil included time at her make-believe dry-cleaning establishment. There she cleaned, pressed, and hung from the back of a ladder-back chair every one of her daddy's button-down oxford-cloth dress shirts. Occasionally an invisible-to-me patron came in and found her family's garments not ready yet. When that happened, Rachel apologized profusely and promised to have the job done by tomorrow.

Rachel loved playing "pharmacy" and "dry cleaner," as well as "Wal-Mart" and "Chinese place." But by far her favorite pretend retail establishment, her most elaborate make-believe setting, was the grocery store—likely because of the abundance of real-life props to be found in our house.

From the low shelves in the kitchen pantry, Rachel would glean canned tuna and spaghetti sauce, unopened jars of mustard and pickles, sacks of flour and cornmeal. She would haul each of her chosen items to—of all places—the bathroom she shared with her older brother. I suppose she picked the odd setting because of the low counter, but who really knows? Once in the bathroom, she'd spread everything out neatly on the counter and along the edge of the tub—bags of dried beans and peas, packages of chips, and boxes of crackers. As store manager, she saw to it that every item was arranged just so. Somehow she always managed to create a tempting display—even in this unlikely setting. A toy cash register I picked up for her at a garage sale and a cache of play money lent authenticity to her venture.

Rachel would play for hours, and I enjoyed watching her. So as not to make her self-conscious, I learned to peek around the corner when she wasn't looking. I'd listen to her interact with make-believe customers and observe her as she rang up their purchases and made change.

What I didn't enjoy was cajoling, reminding, and encouraging her to put everything *back* into the pantry when the game was over. By then she'd be tired and would have lost interest. I'd have to prod her over and over to get the job done. She *hated* returning the items, so she always stalled and made excuses, often only half did the job. Although I supported her creative endeavors, I didn't enjoy having to retrieve the baking powder from the bathroom when I was ready to make biscuits.

One sunny morning, several days since Rachel had last had her store set up, I was stirring up breakfast, planning my day. Suddenly she came running into the kitchen, so wide-eyed and excited she could hardly get her words out.

"Mommy, there's something in my bathroom! Come see!"

I followed her. She was right. Something *was* in her bathroom. Something not intended to be in there. From the drain in the sink sprang the oddest of sights—a tangle of bright-green leafy sprouts—shoots I identified at once as quick-growing pinto bean plants!

So this was why the drain had been sluggish of late!

"Rachel," I questioned her, "did you put beans down the sink?"

She hung her head, stammered and stuttered. Finally, the truth came out. In her hasty efforts to put away the "store," a half-dozen stray beans had escaped their sack. Rather than putting them where they belonged, my little grocery store gal had simply swept them into the sink. Out of sight, out of mind. Right?

Not this time. The moist, dark conditions of the bathroom drain had rapidly produced a crop of healthy little plants.

"Mommy, I'm sorry. I won't do it again. How will I brush my teeth? How will I wash my hands?"

Knowing she was picturing a garden taking over this most important of rooms, I struggled not to giggle. "Not to worry." I hugged her. "It's okay. We can get them out of the sink and plant them in the yard. Want to?"

Of course she did. I could see it now. At this very moment, a plant store was taking shape in my daughter's industrious little brain.

Let's see, she'd need pots and dirt, seeds, a shovel and a trowel, maybe a watering can...

Work for Everyone

Rachel, now in her mid-teens, no longer plays store. She doesn't pretend to take prescriptions over a toy telephone anymore. These days her career aspirations have shifted from the coveted career at Wal-Mart to making plans to become a social worker and help troubled children. I'm proud of her interest in that particular career, but I also realize it's likely that even this noble, mature goal will be replaced many times before she actually enters the workforce.

No matter. The important thing is for Rachel to learn that work is valuable and to understand that she is expected to do whatever job she takes on to the best of her ability. For whatever our daughters end up doing with their lives—whether they become industrious full-time homemakers, part-time workers whose primary goals are to help make family ends meet, or full-fledged career women—we want them to develop good work habits.

And since work often equals pay, we also want them to learn to manage their money. Short-term, part-time jobs provide excellent, hands-on introductions to both.

Jobs for Girls

1. Babysitting—Using a tag-team approach with a girlfriend, then splitting the pay, makes this classic teen money-maker lots more fun. If a daughter is a bit young or if she's not had much experience with children, she can plan to keep her young charges at *her* house, where Mom can offer suggestions and support.

2. Yardwork—Neighbors often need and are willing to pay for help with big seasonal jobs like leaf raking in the fall and flower bed preparation in the spring. Weekly yard maintenance can provide a great source of steady income too. Who says only guys can mow yards?

3. Pet care—Boarding pets for even a few days can be expensive for pet owners. Offering to feed,

water, walk, and play with pets for a reasonable fee can be a great service to vacationing neighbors. An added service might be to bring in the mail and the newspaper.

4. Garage-sale helper—Holding a garage sale is a difficult job for one person. A girl can charge a by-the-hour fee for helping staff neighborhood sales, making change, answering questions, and staying to clean up when the day is over. An added plus—she's likely to pick up a few bargains for herself in the process!
5. Window washer—This twice-a-year job is a task dreaded by most homeowners. A girl unafraid of aching muscles and a soggy T-shirt can arm herself with cleaning supplies and find herself as busy as she wants to be every spring and fall.

Working at jobs like these provides girls the opportunities to learn new skills, as well as responsibility and accountability. Though Mom may choose to hire her own daughter on occasion, when a girl works for someone else, out from under Mom's watchful eye, she gains real-life experiences and insight into the world of work.

Budget Is Not a Bad Word

When a girl begins to enjoy having money of her own, she has the opportunity to learn the basics of money management. Those of us who find ourselves strapped with consumer debt and lacking adequate savings (and from what I've gleaned from talking to scores of women, it's a big sisterhood) understand the importance of our daughters learning these financial skills. We want something better for our girls than what we've created for ourselves. While we take our own steps toward better money management, we can begin early to teach our girls how to manage their spending. A great place to start is with a simple ten-ten-eighty rule:

1. Ten percent to church or charity.
2. Ten percent to savings.
3. Eighty percent to spend.

Providing a girl with three sturdy envelopes, one for each category, creates a practical way for her to keep track of her finances. Whenever she receives money, she is taught to immediately divvy it up among the three envelopes.

On Sunday, she is expected to empty out the "church or charity" envelope. Every six months, or perhaps once a year—after consulting with Mom—she is allowed to spend her "savings" envelope on a bigger-ticket item. As for the "spend" envelope? A daughter is allowed to spend it—or squander it—*any way she chooses.*

Granted, we moms find it painful to watch a daughter spend a week's worth of hard-earned summertime wages on magazines and junk jewelry. We want to throw up our hands when she chooses to spend her own money on an item we would normally provide for her—if she'd just wait until the end of the month. We try to make her understand that the item she insists on purchasing today will be on sale—50 percent off—come Friday. We want to stop her from spending so foolishly.

Too bad for us. For no matter how sore our tongues get from our biting down hard on them, this is the time to let a daughter work it out herself, to discover on her own what happens when money is spent as fast as it's earned. Unfortunately, allowing foolish spending isn't even the hardest part. Much more difficult is the challenge of allowing her to deal with the consequences of her choices. When she's out of money, but finds an item she's wanted badly—like a hard-to-find CD or a hair scrunchie in the perfect difficult-to-match shade of green—sadly, she'll have to pass it up. When her best friend invites her to the mall, she may have to be content with window shopping if she's spent all her money. Only by being allowed to spend as she desires, and by being allowed to do without something she really longs for, does a daughter learn about real life.

To Give or Not to Give

I agree with the experts who advocate giving children an allowance. The system that has worked well for our family is this one: Every year or so (because as she gets older, Rachel's needs do increase) we calculate how much money per month she routinely requires for things like school lunches, club and activity dues, ball-game concessions, school supplies and the like—items we would normally give her money for on a day-to-day basis. To this amount we add a small cushion—a few dollars a week. Totaled up, this equals the amount we give her in a lump sum. When Rachel was younger, she received her allowance once a week. Now that she's older, it's given to her every two weeks. In another year or two, we'll stretch it out to once a month. Our goal is to teach her how to make her money last.

In our family, allowances are not withheld for punishment. (That's what the telephone is for!) Nor are good grades, good behavior, or good attitudes rewarded with allowance increases. Our sole purpose in giving Rachel an allowance is to teach her how to manage her money. Nothing else.

A side benefit to this approach is that no longer do I find myself probing my purse every morning for lunch money, making extra trips to the bank to cash checks, or frantically digging beneath the couch cushions in search of last-minute school-supply money. Giving Rachel her funds on a routine basis has simplified the whole spending process. So far she's done well with the system.

I realized just how well she *has* done when last Saturday I was heading out the door to meet a friend for lunch. At the last minute I found myself with no money.

"Rachel," I asked in my most desperate voice, "I'm out of cash. Can I borrow a few dollars till Monday?"

"Sure, Mom," she barely looked up from her book. "Look in my top drawer, under my notebook."

I headed down the hall toward her room.

"Just one thing. Would you mind leaving me an IOU? You know, in case you forget to pay me back. That way I can keep track."

Like I said—we all hope our daughters will learn the lessons we've missed and do better in almost every way than we've done. I'd say when it comes to money, Rachel is well on her way.

Come, all you who are thirsty, come to the waters;
and you who have no money, come, buy and eat!
Come, buy wine and milk without money and without cost.
Why spend money on what is not bread,
and your labor on what does not satisfy?
Listen, listen to me, and eat what is good,
and your soul will delight in the richest of fare.
Give ear and come to me;
hear me, that your soul may live.

—ISAIAH 55:1-3

Money Lessons

1. When grocery shopping with your daughter, explain to her why you buy certain brands. Show her the cost-per-unit pricing found on the shelf beneath each item. Teach her to compare the costs of competing brands. (Peanut butter provides a dramatic illustration of the way prices vary. Compare the plain store brand to the national brands, and both of them to the fancy stuff that comes already swirled with jelly. Amazing!)

2. When you are saving for something—an article of clothing or an item for the house— let your daughter in on what you're doing. Show her how simply skipping your daily on-the-way-to-work latte helps you reach your goal.

3. Instead of responding, "We can't afford it," to a daughter's questions about finances, explain that choices the family has made affect the way money is spent:

   - "We *choose* to live in a smaller house so I don't have to work full time."
   - "Because we've *chosen* to drive an older car, we are able to go to the beach every summer."

- "Making the *choice* to shop for shorts and T-shirts at the secondhand shop allows us to have more money to spend on new, name-brand athletic shoes."

4. Make charitable giving—beyond the regular tithe—a family project. Send school supplies to an orphanage. Donate groceries to a food pantry. Adopt a needy child at Christmas. Show by your example the lesson that money and things are to be shared with the needy.

9
Girls in Motion

Mom's No Jock

When I was in the first grade, my teacher, Mrs. Flemming, passed out mimeographed forms so we girls could sign up for summer softball. I had never played softball before, in fact, had never even watched a softball game. But my best friend Carla said she was going to play, so I decided I would too.

At least that was my plan. My mom didn't think it was such a good idea. Raised in a different generation and in a non-athletic family, she feared that if I played ball, I would become loud and unladylike. I might in fact become a tomboy.

(And wouldn't that have been awful!)

I was 12 years old before I owned a softball glove. That year, my teacher, as well as the teachers at the four other elementary schools in town, divided us up into teams: boys' A and B teams, girls' A and B teams. Every Friday in spring, we sixth graders boarded steamy yellow school buses and traveled across town to play other teams. My friend Carla, by now a skilled veteran of six years of summer softball, was named pitcher on the A team. I became the reluctant third baseman for my school's B team. Slow, uncoordinated, and scared of the ball, when we were in the outfield I guarded my base and prayed *Dear Jesus, just don't let them hit it to me.* When my team was up to bat, I swung wildly at the first three pitches thrown. *Better to just get it over with* was my philosophy. Not once in my short-lived life as a ballplayer did I hit the ball.

I did not have fun.

When I was in junior high, my mom, by now enlightened about sports and repentant of her previous attitude, signed me up for six weeks of tennis lessons at the city courts. I liked the idea. It was fun picking out a racket, and I got new shoes and terry-cloth socks with little pink and yellow balls on the back. *Tennis is great so far,* I thought. Unfortunately, my optimism ended about ten minutes into my very first lesson. Lacking even a bit of hand-eye coordination, I spent my time chasing balls, getting drinks of water, and counting the weeks till my lessons were over. So seldom did the balls I whacked go over the net and land within the boundaries, I didn't even learn to keep score. There was no need, actually. Without fail, whenever I played, the score was always something-love. And I was love.

Then came high school. Few girls played sports. I remember only one girl I knew who played tennis. Athletic participation for me and most of my friends consisted of hours and hours of committed sunbathing. Don't laugh. There is an art to accomplished tanning. It's a difficult challenge, once a girl is greased with lotion, for her to manage to turn completely over without rolling off her towel. It takes firm concentration and lots of practice. Try it. You'll see.

As an adult, I still lack coordination and skill. I am terrible at sports—all sports. I tried tennis again as an adult, and I even attempted golf—once. I hated both. Admittedly, I am a couch potato. But because I know physical activity is conducive to both a healthy body and a clear mind, I walk. Not as often as I should. Not as far as I should. Never as fast as I should. But at least it's something.

Besides, every so often I get to buy new shoes and cute colored socks.

Things Have Changed

Thankfully, Rachel's athletic experiences have been nothing like mine. She began playing softball at age five, the same year as her brother. Since junior high, Rachel has participated in every girl's sport available to her: track, basketball, and volleyball. If we lived in a larger town, and other sports such as soccer, swimming, tennis, or golf were offered, I have no doubt that she would be involved in them too.

Rachel inherited a fair amount of coordination and athletic ability from her dad. She has never been a star player, but she has a achieved a high enough level of skill and physical fitness to allow her to enjoy playing.

Rachel's dad played sports when he was growing up and has in fact made them his livelihood. In his work as a high-school girls' coach, he sees firsthand the benefits of athletic participation. Randy believes that the lessons girls learn about discipline, responsibility, and teamwork carry over into their academic lives, their peer relationships, and their feelings about themselves.

Why Sports for Girls?

Why should girls play sports? If my mother had realized the benefits of playing sports, it's likely she would have been my biggest first-grade fan. Girls who play sports do better in school, have higher self-esteem, and have a better body image.

Teen female athletes become pregnant less often than do nonathletes. Girls who focus on fitness in order to perform well are less likely to smoke or use alcohol or illegal drugs. Anxiety and depression, common in adolescent girls, is reduced by physical activity. Nothing relieves stress like a good sweat! Regular physical activity also reduces a girl's risk of obesity.

When girls are required to make good grades (either by parents, coaches, or league rules) in order to remain on a team, their motivation for academic success increases. When girls play sports, they learn to set goals, to think strategically, and to strive for excellence. These skills will help them as they pursue higher education and will be of great benefit in the workplace.

Participation in sports encourages girls to focus on what their bodies can *do,* rather than on how they *look.* Athletic apparel, while colorful and attractive, is designed for performance and comfort rather than fad and fashion. During athletic participation, when a girl pulls her hair into a ponytail, forgets the makeup, and dresses for freedom of movement instead of style, she's learning that she's acceptable and valuable even without all the feminine trappings that society and the media tell her are necessary for good looks.

Encouraging Them to Play

The number one reason girls give for playing sports is enjoyment. They like to have fun! And it is success that makes participation enjoyable. While most daughters will be average players, not stars, every girl can be encouraged to be the best she can be. Help a daughter develop skill in her chosen sport by making sure she attends all practices. If she desires additional help, enlist an older teenager to help her improve her skill. Be sure she has the equipment she needs.

Winning and losing should be kept in perspective. Emphasize the importance of personal improvement, even when a contest is lost. A daughter's self-worth shouldn't be tied to her performance, but to her efforts.

Take girls to watch older teams play. High-school games and meets are inexpensive and readily available. These events give young girls a chance to see more skilled teen athletes in action. Attending a professional women's sporting event is a great outing to plan with another mother and her daughter or with the whole family, Dad and brothers included.

With dozens of sports now available, there is at least one suited to every girl. She may be bored by basketball but love fencing. If she's a slow runner, track probably won't interest her, but she may love kick boxing. If she hates to sweat, swimming may be just the thing. Aerobic dance may appeal to her more than mountain biking, tennis more than skating. The point is that whether she is coordinated or clumsy, high-energy or low, with effort and experimentation any girl can find *some* athletic activity that interests her.

Cheering Them On

I confess. Displaying appropriate enthusiasm for whatever team Rachel may be playing on is not always easy for me. Born with a noncompetitive personality, I don't get as excited and worked up about the games as other mothers do. I wish I did, but I admit that it just doesn't come naturally for me. While I have never wavered in my belief in the value of sports, I have had to *work* at becoming a true fan.

Watching the ways other mothers support their girls, I've learned to back my own daughter in ways that let her know how proud I am of her athletic endeavors. Honestly, there's not that much to it. Support starts with just going to the games or exhibitions. Girls *love* knowing that Mom is watching and cheering them on—even if they don't play or perform exceptionally well. My mother-in-law, Dorothy, who raised three student athletes, explains it like this: "If one of my children was going to score a point, I wanted to be there to see it. But even if the most exciting thing to happen to them during a game was that they got a splinter in their behind from sitting on the bench, well, I didn't want to miss that either!"

Moms can support their daughters by attending every game possible, wearing the team colors, and yelling really loudly!

A Place to Belong

Athletic participation can give shy or reticent girls an instant, generally positive peer group. Sports create an easy way to make friends and fit in. Strong bonds form between teammates who otherwise wouldn't even know each other. Through athletic participation girls make friends with girls of different ethnic groups, from different economic levels, and with different interests. Every opportunity a girl has to forge healthy bonds with other girls helps develop her personality and her sense of self.

Someone to Look Up To

While the media gives great attention to scandals over coaches who behave inappropriately, for the most part the men and women who coach student athletes do so for two reasons: They love both the kids and the game. Coaches can be great role models for girls. In the midst of a busy season, when a coach holds practices both during and after school, a girl will spend as much if not more time with her coach than she will with her parents.

Often, during tumultuous times at home, a daughter will listen to words of wisdom from her coach while ignoring the same admonishments from her parents. Every girl benefits from associations with adults—in addition to her parents—who care for her and have her best interests at heart.

During the 18 years he's spent coaching, my husband Randy has watched many awkward little girls grow up to be graceful, confident young women. He's coached long enough now that when former players stop by to visit, they often do so with their own little girls in tow. More than just their coach, he has been a friend, a confidant, and a mentor to many, many student athletes.

Randy has collected lots of pictures and memorabilia over the years. He saves the letters and cards and notes he's received from players. They are all special to him. One of the notes, sent to him by a lonely young athlete, illustrates beautifully what an impact a coach can have on a girl. Since the message was meant for him alone, I've changed enough details so as not to reveal the student's identity:

> *Coach Smith,*
>
> *Would it be all right if I missed practice Thursday? We are supposed to go see a counselor. We just had a big blow-up at my house. I really do need the counseling and I'll make up what I miss at practice.*
>
> *One more thing. My mom and I were talking and your name got mentioned and she made me realize something. I asked her why she thought that you were such a caring person, even to your athletes. She said, "Well he's a father, has a heart, and knows Christ." I thought about it awhile. I realized that for the past few months you became and still are my father figure. You're everything that I've wanted in a father, but I never had one like that.*
>
> *So like it or not, you've got another teenager looking up to you. Thank you for being there for me.*
>
> *Love,*
> *A student*

Randy and I ran into this former student recently. Her eyes sparkled as she told us about her part-time job, her new apartment, and her classes at the university. As she spoke, she held on tightly to the hand of her new husband.

"She's going to be fine," Randy casually observed as we watched the two of them walk away.

"Yes, it looks like she is," I agreed. *Thanks in part to you, Coach.*

In Honor of Them All

My friend Toni introduced me to the world of competitive 5K and 10K runs and walks. A well-trained runner, she has participated in many of these events over the years. It was at her urging that Rachel and I signed up to participate in a big charity walk benefiting breast cancer research. It would be fun, she told me. We'd drive down the night before, do some shopping, stay in a hotel. Besides, the event was six months away, and it would be good motivation to get in shape.

And so we did. Night after night, month after month, Toni and Rachel and I met at the high-school track. We counted our laps and lengthened our strides and improved our speed and endurance. We got ourselves in shape!

The springtime event took place in a beautiful area where the streets were lined with lovely homes boasting gorgeous, well-tended flower gardens. The weather was spectacular—warm and sunny, yet not too hot. More than a thousand women showed up to support the cause. Old women, young women, fast and fit women, plump and puffing women—all marched together. I remember I liked the feeling that the three of us were part of a bigger sisterhood united against a common, destructive foe.

The day was exciting and exhausting and full of emotional vignettes that were very moving. Women in wheelchairs wore protective gloves and propelled themselves up every hill and around every curve. Women with twisted ankles and swollen knees were urged to quit, but wouldn't, and instead kept limping ahead, determined to finish with the rest of us.

Pink was everywhere. Poignant were the hundreds of women who wore bright pink visors that identified them as breast cancer survivors. Sobering were the walkers who sported pink paper banners pinned to their T-shirts...*I walk in memory of Cynthia Jones...Stacie McKinzie...Olivia Barnes*...each woman a sore-muscled symbol of personal loss. Encouraging were the walkers who wore banners acknowledging loved ones' cautious victories over the disease...*I walk in celebration of Margaret Phillips...Maggie Majors...Patricia Patterson...*

About halfway through the race I spotted a mother and daughter up ahead who looked to be about the same age as Rachel and me. They were both wearing pink banners, and curious, I struggled and sped up enough to read what they said. When I was able to, the words I saw broke my heart. On the woman's banner: *I walk in memory of my mother;* on the little girl's: *I walk in memory of Grandma.*

My eyes burned with sweat and tears, but I wiped at them and kept on walking. And as Rachel caught up with me, I gave her a weary smile, and I breathed a silent prayer: *Thank you, God, for health and for life.*

May we always be grateful.

Do you not know that in a race all the runners run,
but only one gets the prize?
Run in such a way as to get the prize.
Everyone who competes in the games goes into strict training.
They do it to get a crown that will not last;
but we do it to get a crown that will last forever.

—1 Corinthians 9:24,25

Encourage Her to Try

1. Brainstorm with your daughter about a new sport or athletic activity the two of you can try together. Suggestions: skating, hiking, biking, water aerobics, or aerobic dance.

2. On gift-giving occasions, purchase sports-related presents such as an optional but fun piece of equipment or gear, a poster or a book about a famous female athlete, or tickets to a professional game.

3. Model good exercise habits yourself. If you've been sedentary for awhile, discuss with your daughter why you wish to get in shape. Share with her your struggles, your progress, and how you're feeling stronger and more fit.

10
Look Both Ways

Trouble at the Quick Stop

Quiet, mild-mannered Larry is the faithful husband of my friend Olivia and the tender father of their two children, Rena and Josh. Larry goes to work every day, pays his taxes on time, coaches Little League baseball in the summer, and sings every Sunday in the Combined Adult Choir at the large church he and Olivia attend. Larry has no vices that I can think of, and possesses but one amusing personality quirk: He is incredibly easy to embarrass.

Which pretty much explains why he nearly throttled six-year-old Rena recently at the local Quick Stop. Who could have predicted it? The ill-fated Saturday morning episode started out as a routine convenience-store pit stop. The two of them had spent the morning running errands. Larry needed to fill the car up with gas, and Rena had told him she needed to use the bathroom. Both of them were hungry for a snack, and clear of the watchful eye of wife and mom, Olivia (the woman makes a divine fat-free carrot-carob-apple muffin), the two of them salivated at the realization they could pick out any greasy, artificially colored, preservative-polluted goodie they craved.

And so they did. Larry chose crispy pork rinds, barbecue-spiced peanuts, and a real (not diet) Coke. Rena picked out pink snowball snack cakes, Starburst candies, and a Yoo-Hoo chocolate drink.

Patiently clutching their calorie-laden loot, the pair waited to check out. Near noon, the store was full of hungry shoppers. At the front of the line, a pair of young men, conspicuously tidy in dark slacks and buttoned-to-the-neck long-sleeved white shirts, (Mormon missionaries, Larry decided) paid for turkey sandwiches and orange juice. Behind the young men, directly in front of Larry and Rena, a muscular, pony-tailed man dressed in bikers' black leather rested sweaty six-packs of *his* favorite beverage against ample thighs. To the rear of Larry and Rena waited two elderly women that Larry recognized—but for the life of him could not name—from church. Not yet in line, still perusing the store's snack selection, were eight members of the local Girl Scout Troop #66. The uniformed girls stood and chattered importantly about recycling, debated which was more earth-friendly: chips in a bag or crackers in a box.

Easygoing Larry, credit card in hand, took it all in and stood patiently, waiting his turn to pay for the gas and their snacks.

It was at this most opportune of times that Rena, a proud first-grader, chose to demonstrate her newly acquired academic skills. "B-e-e-r. B-e-e-r. Beer." Rena painstakingly sounded out the label on biker man's beverage. Suddenly her eyes widened, and she tugged on Larry's sleeve. "Daddy! That big man is buying beer!"

"Rena, shhhh," Larry hissed.

"But Daddy! Beer is BAD! My teacher said."

Big biker man, his back still toward them, shifted from one foot to the other. Larry thought he saw the man's multi-tattooed arm muscles flex.

"That's right, Rena," Larry bent down and whispered, his face growing hot, "but let's talk about it when we get home. Okay?"

"Okay. But Daddy, you used to drink beer didn't you?"

Larry felt the church ladies' eyes on the back of his neck.

"No, honey," he spoke deliberately. "You know I don't drink beer. I drink Coke."

The missionaries were staring. Larry could feel it. They were probably praying.

"But Daddy, remember when you and Uncle Mason used to drink beer?"

One beer. *How could she possibly remember?* He'd drank one beer. Two years ago. Had impulsively shared it with his brand-new brother-in-law. He didn't even like the stuff, and besides that one and only can, he could count on one hand the number of *sips* of alcohol he'd consumed in his *whole* life.

"Daddy, I'm sure glad you *finally* quit drinking," Rena continued. "Mommy's *really* glad too."

Larry felt like he was drowning in a sea of eavesdropping green. Girl Scouts were everywhere. Listening to every word. Didn't they have merit badges to earn or something?

"I'm *so* proud of you, Daddy."

"I'm-proud-of-you-too-Rena-get-in-the-car-right-now."

"Okay, Daddy. I sure do love you, Daddy."

"I love you too, Rena. Buckle up."

In Agreement

Know anyone like Larry? You probably do. We Christians hold a variety of beliefs about drinking. On this controversial issue, firmly held opinions, ideas, and convictions vary widely. Many believers hold to the conviction that it's wrong for a Christian to *ever* drink alcohol. Others believe that, though the Bible condemns drunkenness, occasional responsible consumption is perfectly fine. I confess that when I study the issue, sometimes I come up with more questions than answers.

Is all drinking wrong?

Always wrong?

Can it be wrong for me, but okay for you?

Many mothers find themselves unsure about the answers to tough questions like these. Uncomfortably we wonder: *If groups of intelligent, faithful adults are unable to decide on the morality of drinking, how can we mothers possibly expect to teach our daughters about it?* Is it possible?

Absolutely. For no matter how muddled our own beliefs may be regarding adults who drink, this fact is a sure one. *Drinking is never, ever okay for children.*

Rachel's dad and I tell her that some adults, Christians who we love and respect, choose to drink. Others believe drinking is wrong. We use information, Scripture, and family history to explain to her our own views about drinking. When she's an adult, we tell her, we will expect her to study and pray and develop her own convictions. Hopefully she'll reach the same conclusions we've reached. Perhaps she won't. But this fact we stress: *She is legally a child, and children do not have a choice. Children do not drink.* In our state, Texas, a girl is considered a child until she is 21. *End of story.*

Up in Smoke

Many moms believe that smoking is less a problem for girls than for boys. Not so. Adolescent girls are the only population group whose smoking has increased over the past 20 years. This fact has not escaped tobacco advertisers. Ads aimed at young women abound in the media. Our daughters are prime targets.

Why so?

Many adolescent girls long to be older than their actual ages. They want to appear sophisticated and mature. Though the sight of a group of barely-teens smoking appears to be anything *but* sophisticated to us adults, adolescents don't see it that way. Smoking, forbidden and dangerous, lends some girls a feeling of power and independence. It also buys acceptance into certain peer groups.

Rachel tells me she has never been tempted to smoke. She finds the smell of it repulsive. Not only does the aroma of a lit cigarette sicken her, she also dislikes the stink present on the clothing and breath of smokers. Why, she wonders, would anyone want to smoke?

Why indeed? Isn't the smell of cigarette smoke offensive to most if not all nonsmokers? Rare would be the young girl who begins smoking because she thinks she'll enjoy it, because she craves the smell or taste. And the health risks associated with smoking are taught to girls from kindergarten on. Today, it would be impossible for a girl to start smoking ignorant of its dangers.

Like Rachel, I wasn't tempted to smoke during my teen years. How is it that though we grew up a generation apart, in households that differed greatly, tobacco use appealed to neither of us? What do the two of us have in common? One similarity is obvious: My close friends didn't smoke. Neither do Rachel's. If my girlfriends had been smokers, it's likely that I would have tried it too. The same would likely hold true for Rachel.

Put Together a Plan

Moms can help their daughters make good choices by outlining strategies they can use if confronted with an offer to smoke, drink alcohol, or use drugs. Rachel tells me that if a girl makes it plain—and it only takes saying "no" a few times, she assures me—for the most part, peers will stop asking. Rachel tells me that there are parties and gatherings to which she is not invited. It's not because she lacks popularity, but because the hosts of the party know that these gatherings are not ones she would choose to attend.

Girls need to be told that we don't expect them to convert others to their way of thinking, nor do we expect them to police their friends. They need to know that simply saying "no thanks" is usually enough. While it may seem inappropriate to be discussing such issues with nine- or ten-year-olds, this truly is the age that girls are making decisions about their future behavior.

Our daughters need to know they can call us anytime, from anywhere, if they find themselves in an unsafe or uncomfortable situation. Rachel and I have come up with the following plan: If she finds herself in a difficult situation and is unsure how to get herself out of it, she will pretend to suddenly become ill. She will call home, and either I or her dad will come pick her up. Rachel hasn't yet had to use this ploy, but having a plan gives her safety and power. Mothers and daughters can come up with their own plans. Now is the time to discuss them.

Let There Be No Doubt

Let's face it—these are the years when our daughters begin to lead lives that are increasingly independent of us. No longer are our girls under the watchful eyes of adults every minute of every day. In these years they will begin going to parties, participating in school-sponsored off-campus activities, and taking church youth group trips. Perhaps they will spend time visiting out-of-town relatives without us. Great! Enriching activities such as these help our daughters grow into healthy, self-assured young women.

With every year, a girl's freedoms and responsibilities should increase. This organized process prepares her for adulthood. However, with increasing independence come greater opportunities for problems—serious problems.

Rarely is it considered appropriate to throw what we mothers here in the South call a "fit." Most misbehavior merits a more reserved approach. However, the discovery of a daughter's experimentation with alcohol, tobacco, or drugs is exactly the time to exercise a mother's right to have one. A big one. Take firm action. Let her know in no uncertain terms that such behavior will not be tolerated. State reasons for your opposition clearly. Seek the advice of professionals quickly if homegrown efforts to deal with the problem don't produce results.

Peer relationships have *everything* to do with a girl's behavior. If a daughter is engaging in unacceptable activities, it's almost a sure thing that she's involved with a negative peer group. No matter what a daughter may say or perceive, the truth is that *everyone is not doing it.* Though some schools and communities have an alarmingly high incidence of tobacco, alcohol, and drug use, in every school, in every city or town, there always exist groups of students who choose not to participate in such behaviors.

Bottom line? She should be removed from the negative peer group. During the years of young adolescence it is possible and entirely appropriate to inform a girl that she is no longer allowed to associate with certain groups or individuals. Obviously, monitoring a daughter's friendships at school can be difficult, but she can be prohibited from any out-of-school contact, including talks on the telephone. If this approach is required, she will need guidance in finding new friends. When a daughter counters that disconnecting from her old friends will leave her with *no friends,* she may be telling the painful truth.

She will likely be both angry and lonely, and she will need lots of help finding new friends. Mom can help her become engaged in after-school activities such as volunteering, art, music, or theater. In some cases changing schools may be the best option. Home-schooling should be considered.

Though these measures may sound harsh and uncompromising, when the issue is substance abuse, a daughter's very life hangs in the balance. The dangers of alcohol and drug abuse cannot be overstated. The younger a girl is when she begins experimenting with chemicals, the greater the chance she will develop a full-blown addiction or dependency. Moms, dads, extended families, churches, schools, and communities must have the courage to take whatever measures are necessary to stop a girl from being harmed by the effects of tobacco, alcohol, and drugs.

All Too Common

For the past several years my work has allowed me to serve as camp nurse at a therapeutic wilderness program for troubled girls, ages 12 to 17. Thirty to 35 emotionally disturbed girls live at the secluded, rustic camp for stretches ranging from six months to one year. While there, they attend school, receive counseling, and through participating in group dynamics learn valuable coping skills. In my daily routine I assess the girls' general health, refer them to a physician when the need arises, and monitor their medications.

Last month, I called Tina (not her real name), a new client who I'd not yet met, into my office. I needed to check her height and her weight. After I'd introduced myself, I told her what we were doing, and she stepped on the scale.

"Nurse," she spoke while I measured her height, "can I ask you a question?"

"Sure, babe, what's going on?" Tina seemed bright and cheerful and unusually at ease.

When she confided to me symptoms of a sexually transmitted disease, my response was well practiced: I asked whether she'd had unprotected sex, and when.

Suddenly her bright face crumpled, and a chilling story unfolded. There had been a rape. Several months before her arrival at camp, she and her sister had stood on a street corner in their hometown, attempting to sell drugs. When a man in a gold car approached them, Tina willingly climbed in to make the sale. The man told her they'd take a drive and then he'd make his purchase. Instead he took her to a secluded spot, beat her, raped her, and attempted to run over her with his car.

Until this moment, she had shared her experience with no one.

I am well trained—good at what I do—but I could take all the courses in the world, read a library full of books, and sit through hours of specialized training, and still come up unprepared for moments like this one.

I took her in my arms and I let her cry. I stroked her hair and I rubbed her back and I told her she was a precious, precious little girl and that I was so, so, sorry this had happened to her. After she was cried out, I wiped her face and I bought her a soda and hugged her again before sending her back to her group.

Then, as I've done so many times before, I cleared my throat, closed my office door, and did my job. I filed the necessary crime report, and I scheduled Tina for an examination and treatment by a compassionate gynecologist. I arranged everything I could to the best of my ability. What I could not do was fix what was broken in Tina's young life.

Drugs and violence are facts of our modern society. How does a girl, a *child* like 13-year-old Tina, come to the place that selling drugs on a street corner is a normal way of life? How do we keep such things from happening to our own precious girls?

I offer no easy answers.

I *am* convinced that children need our love, our faith, and our *diligence.* We cannot let our guards down for even a minute. We must do everything we can to protect them, to encourage them, to teach them to make good decisions.

They are worth it.

Tina is too.

They are more precious than gold,
than much pure gold.
—PSALM 19:10

Let's Talk

1. Spend an hour with your daughter looking at advertisements in magazines. Begin with ads for cosmetics, cleaning products, and cars. Ask her whether she thinks the products featured in the ads can really do what they promise. Then study ads for tobacco products and alcoholic beverages. Talk about how consumers don't get the true picture of the effects of the products. Ask her how she thinks the ads affect teenagers.

2. When the story of a drunk-driving accident, especially one involving teenagers, is featured on the news or in the paper, talk to your daughter about it. Discuss the tragic consequences of the decisions made by people very much like her.

3. Discuss situations your daughter might face in a few years, such as being offered a wine cooler at a party or being the only one at a slumber party reluctant to try smoking. Role-play the entire situation, with Mom being the "bad kid" and your daughter being herself.

Some Disturbing Facts

According to a recent report by the U.S. Department of Health and Human Services, adolescent female use of alcohol, tobacco, and illicit drugs rose during the 1990s. For example:

- Nearly 20 percent of girls smoke cigarettes.
- Nearly 20 percent drink alcoholic beverages.
- Almost one in ten girls in this age group reports using an illicit drug within the past month.
- Eighth-grade girls (13- and 14-year-olds) use drugs at approximately the same rates as boys. The rate of use increases sharply as girls move into the later years of adolescence.

Keeping Them Safe

A publication titled *Keeping Youth Drug-Free: A Guide for Parents, Grandparents, Elders, Mentors, and other Caregivers,* published by the Center for Substance Abuse Prevention, may be obtained by calling 800-729-6686 or by contacting the Center's website at http://www.health.org.

Risk Factors

Factors that can contribute to substance abuse among adolescents (from the National Institute on Drug Abuse):

- Chaotic home environment in which parents abuse substances or suffer from mental illness
- Disadvantaged environment
- Poor academic performance
- Aggressive and impulsive personality traits
- Deviant peer influence
- Availability of alcohol and other drugs
- Belief that substance use is the norm
- Ineffective parenting
- Lack of mutual attachments

Protective Factors

Factors that can help avert addiction:

- Strong family bonds
- Involvement of parents in the lives of their children
- Success in school
- Adoption of attitudes that are critical of drug use

11
Daddy's Girl

ALWAYS THE BEST

Cherry Ames, America's First Trained Nurse was my favorite book when I was in the third grade. I fell in love with the heroine's dedication, with her spunk, and with her devotion to caring for the ill and injured.

When I was 17 years old, I began working in the laboratory of my town's small community hospital. It was fun, but I didn't want to be a lab tech. I wanted to be a nurse. Problem was, so did a whole bunch of other students. Every year, most of the applicants to the junior college–based nursing school close to my home were turned away. There simply weren't enough slots—which made the competition for admission fierce.

I'll always be grateful to my high-school vocational teacher, Mr. Bennett. He made several phone calls for me, told me who to go see, and somehow managed to convince the admissions folks that, despite my barely B-minus average, they should let me into their school. When I learned of my acceptance into the program, I actually began to believe that, like my old friend Cherry, I too would become a nurse.

My mother and my grandma were thrilled at the news.

My dad was happy for me too, but his initial response was not the same as theirs. "Annette," he advised, blithely unconcerned about my limited academic abilities and my barely average SAT score, "if you're going to be a nurse, why not go on and be a doctor?"

Randy and I married the same week I finished nursing school. Just ten days after the wedding, on a whim we rented a U-Haul trailer, packed up our wedding gifts, and moved to the mountains of Colorado. (We'd heard it was pretty there. Why do 20-year-olds do *any* of the things they do?) We found an apartment and set about to secure employment. It was at a bustling metropolitan teaching hospital where I—a brand-new, just-registered, fresh-out-of-school, wet-behind-the-ears 20-year-old nurse—went to work.

One week after I'd started, my dad and I spoke on the phone. "How's your new job?" he asked.

"Great, Dad. I love it. I'm learning so much. You see, they have this six-month mentoring program for new graduate nurses..."

"So," he interrupted, "are you the Head Nurse?"

I stifled a giggle. The hospital where I'd been hired a mere *seven days* before, employed almost 300 nurses—experienced nurses, professionals who held long strings of degrees and maintained multiple advanced-practice certifications. "Uh, Dad, there are a lot of experienced nurses who work at the hospital, and I'm just barely out of school..."

"But you're the one in charge when you're there, right?"

I was so excited I could barely talk. "Dad, you're not going to believe this, but there's a company that wants me to write a book. You see, I sent them my proposal and they liked it and they say they want to publish it! Dad, they're even going to pay me what they call an advance. It's like, a *lot* of money, Dad. It's even enough that I'm finally going to buy—"

"Why, sure they are," he didn't let me finish. "So you're going to be a writer. When will you tell your boss that you're leaving your nursing job? You want to be sure to give adequate notice, you know."

"—a new mattress for our bed. Maybe even box springs to go with it."

In the forty-plus years since I was born, no one has championed my abilities, believed in my competence, like my dad. Though I sometimes think he must suffer from delusions of grandeur about his children, his unwavering faith in my personal greatness has influenced my life more than he'll ever know. Thanks, Dad!

Unpack Your Bags

Don't we all drag the baggage of our childhood into the middle of the families we create? It's hard not to. Good or bad, we remember how things were when *we* were little girls. We recall how *we* felt about our dads. However, our girls *will not* have the same childhoods we did. They aren't the same as we are, and their dads aren't the same as our dads. Difficult though it may be, we need to let go of our expectations and assumptions. Our girls' dads won't make the same mistakes our dads did; they'll make ones of their own. They won't display the same parenting skills our fathers did, but they'll excel in areas unique to them.

There's No Mom like a Dad

Maybe we're the best mother on the block. Perhaps someday we'll win an award because we're Mother of the Year. Maybe our daughter and all her friends think we're the coolest mom in the world. *We can do it all,* we think. Nope. Sorry. It doesn't work that way. No matter how good we moms are at doing our jobs, none of our efforts will ever be enough to take the place of what our daughters get from their dads.

Funny thing. Dads come in all shapes, sizes, types, and temperaments. Some of them bond instantly with their daughters, others find the relationships with their girls to be slippery and difficult. Some dads dedicate themselves to their families, others spend too much time at work. Some are loud and aggressive in their parenting styles, others are quiet and tend to be too passive about things that really *do* matter. Some dads are strict disciplinarians, others are frankly pushovers.

Some dads stay married to their daughters' mothers. Some don't.

What's a mom to do?

Work with what she's got. Help him be the best dad he can be. Give up the myth of the "perfect" father. (Didn't we, after all, long ago give up on the idea that we could be the "perfect" mother?) Help him to understand his daughter. Guide, orchestrate, and support him in his efforts to parent his little girl, the one who all of a sudden *isn't so little* anymore.

Our efforts are worth it. A girl's relationship with her dad determines, to a great extent, how she'll relate to men all her life. It will affect her dating relationships, her interactions with men in the workplace, and ultimately the way she relates to her own husband. A healthy, secure, relaxed relationship with Dad gives a girl the feeling she's competent, valuable, and worthy of respect. It arms her with a self-esteem that helps protect her from promiscuity and heartbreak. If she's secure in her dad's love, she's less likely to seek out unhealthy, inappropriate affirmations from other men.

Respect Starts with Mom

Watching even an hour or two of prime-time television quickly leads one to believe that all American dads are stupid, lazy, and completely incompetent. TV fathers are most often portrayed as nothing more than drags on their families, of no value to their wives and children—save for a good laugh. In show after show, even our favorite "family-friendly" ones, we see disrespect for Dad being the common theme. If we're not careful, we moms can fall into the habit of treating our husbands in the same patronizing, disrespectful way. When we do so, we can be sure that our daughters are watching.

No matter what may be the faults and flaws of our daughter's daddy, whether he is a good husband, a bad husband, even an ex-husband, he is worthy of our treating him respectfully (though of course if he is abusive, or is an addict, or is otherwise dangerous to us or our girls, we will have to keep him away from us). The way we speak *to* him and *about* him teaches our daughters to be either open, honest, and loving with their dads, or deceitful, manipulative, and cold.

What's a Dad to Do?

Many a dad finds his daughter's adolescence to be a confusing, uncomfortable time. Gone is the little girl in footie pajamas who crawled up in his lap for a cuddle. In her place is a prickly, unpredictable, long-legged beauty who spends hours in the bathroom and wants to learn to drive. No wonder a dad pulls back from his girl during these years. She can be scary!

Moms can help with the transition by letting Dad in on what's happening behind a daughter's closed door. He may have trouble realizing that her growing up behavior is normal. It may be difficult for him to admit that his baby girl isn't a baby anymore. Tell him how she's developing, both physically and emotionally. Assure him she's right on track. Point out other girls her age so he can note how they look, how they behave.

When his old manner of relating to her no longer fits, encourage Dad to adapt to her new maturity. Though her lap-sitting days may be over, she still needs hugs and pats. Though she may no longer play dress-up and ask, "Daddy, do you think I'm pretty?" she longs for him to tell her she is. Even if the two of them have seemingly nothing in common, she still wants him to be interested in her day.

Healing Circle

My friend Jacie was a daddy's girl from the second she was born. Though her dad, turned papa late in life, left the feeding and diapering of infant Jacie to her mother, when playtime came around, he was the man. Over his head he'd lift his tiny daughter, would gaze into her eyes, make her laugh, tickle her tummy, and tease her toes. Worn out from play, every night of her life Jacie went to sleep draped over her daddy's sturdy shoulder.

When she was a toddler, Jacie began to go places with her dad. In those pre–seat belt days, she rode many a mile standing on the seat beside him—stiff-legged, her chubby baby arm wrapped tightly around his neck. He was a careful driver, steady-footed, and not once did she tumble forward.

Because she was such a portable, easygoing child, her dad took her with him almost everywhere—to the pasture, the feed store, the post office—and the coffee shop. It was there, at Sal's Sit-n-Sip, that local farmers gathered for unfiltered Camels, afternoon gossip, and bottomless cups of steaming hot joe. Jacie would sit among the kind gentlemen—the ones who gave her nickels and quarters and bought her gum from the machine by the door—and silently sip her chocolate milk. Over the rim of a two-fisted turned-up glass, her solemn, thickly-lashed brown eyes took everything in. When she'd get tired, lulled by the rhythm of low male voices, she'd fall asleep, slumped and sweaty, against her daddy's lean side.

When she went to elementary school, Jacie's dad missed her terribly but adjusted as best he could. He'd scramble around while she was gone, striving to get most of his on-the-farm work done in the mornings so as to save any errands for the two of them to do in the afternoon. Each day when the last school bell rang, Jacie would run out the door to find her daddy's red pickup truck waiting for her at the curb. He'd look at her papers, comment on her coloring, and take her to the Dairy Queen for an afternoon snack. If the place wasn't busy, Leon, the establishment's 70-year-old bachelor owner, would come to their table, domino box in hand, and ask if perchance Jacie wanted to play.

She beat him nine games out of ten.

The day Jacie turned 12, after candles and cake, she did as she did every day. She took her coat from its hook and made herself ready for an afternoon of errands with Dad. They'd need to hurry, she knew, to get to the post office before it closed. But he was slow today, lingered longer than usual, stalled in the back bedroom, kept talking to Mother.

A birthday surprise? Jacie wondered.

Finally Daddy came and rested his hand on her shoulder. Yes, there was to be a birthday surprise. In a gruff voice, Jacie's dad told her he was sorry, but she wouldn't be going with him anymore.

No understanding. Stunned confusion. *Why, Daddy?*

Her mother tried to explain things for her poor fidgeting husband. Now that Jacie was becoming a young woman, it wasn't right for her to be with the men anymore. Wasn't proper. She understood. Didn't she?

Of course she didn't, but suddenly oddly embarrassed, Jacie folded her arms across her chest and nodded obedience.

That's Daddy's girl.

A single salty tear. Wiped away quickly. Then he left out the door.

Things were never the same after that birthday. Her daddy was still kind and gentle, but from then on, though they could talk about anything, he seemed to hold his beloved daughter at arm's length. Though it was never spoken of, Jacie was left with the nagging feeling that she'd done something terribly wrong. It was a feeling she'd be unable to shake.

Today, my grown-up friend has two children of her own—five-year-old twin girls, Jan and Laura. She and her family live in the same small town where she grew up.

Jacie's daddy is crazy about the little girls. They are his companions of choice, and he hauls them, buckled into the back seat of a new Ford van, all over town. He somehow always finds some important reason that explains his running them by the senior citizen center on the average of twice a week. The girls love to go (they get candy and gum), and so Jacie indulges his unconvincing ruse, stifles a grin at today's creative excuse. She knows he's just looking for a reason to show off his incredibly wonderful granddaughters to his arthritic card-playing cronies.

On this summer day, he picks the girls up after breakfast, takes them with him for the day. They have a plan. The three of them will shop for bird seed at the Farmers' Co-op, purchase vitamins and flip-flops at Walgreen's, and will eat, as they do every time they're together, at McDonalds. Happy Meals. All three of them.

Jacie watches as her dad buckles the girls up, slings the van's sliding door shut, then sprints round the back to hop in the driver's side. If anything, he seems younger and more spry in these his years of retirement. Nothing gives her more joy than seeing the three of them together.

Jacie waves as they drive away, and as she does, one salty little tear falls. As she wipes it away, she also wipes away yet a tiny bit more of 12-year-old hurt. She didn't do anything wrong. She knows it.

If he could, her daddy would tell her so himself.

And the woman was healed from that moment.

—MATTHEW 9:22

Daddy-Daughter Dates

1. Surprise your daughter and her dad with tickets to a big-league sporting event. On the day of the game, present them with matching team caps and coupons for her favorite fast-food meal to enjoy before the game.

2. Take candid photos of the two of them. Frame copies of the same print—one for his office, one for her room.

3. If it's a good one, tell your daughter the story of how her dad acted when he learned she was to be born, and how he behaved when you were in labor. Describe the look on his face the first time he saw her. Tell her how he cared for her when she was little, how it scared him when she was sick.

4. Occasionally leave Dad and daughter home alone in the evening. Instead of preparing and leaving a meal for them, suggest they go out to eat.

5. When Dad goes on a trip for business or pleasure, be sure he carries his daughter's T-shirt size in his wallet. Even a dad with no knowledge of teen fashion can generally manage the selection of a souvenir shirt. She'll enjoy the surprise and be touched that he thought of her.

12

Seeds of Kindness

MIRACLES GROW

Our friend Mac was coming for a visit. It had been more than three years since we'd seen him, but happily, he'd be arriving at our house around six o'clock this very fall evening. Randy was especially eager to see his old high-school buddy. The two of them share a common small-town history, but these days their lives are carried out a couple of hundred miles apart. There was some catching up to be done. Wives, kids, jobs, successes, setbacks—Mac and Randy had a lot to talk about. (Not to mention, of course, the scores and memorable plays from last night's ball game—Randy and Mac *are,* after all, guys!)

Our house is small. With one cozy living area, it offers no good place to carry on a private chat. I knew it would make it easier for the two of them to talk if they had our home to themselves, so once I finished putting their steak and potato dinners on the table, Russell and Rachel and I were planning to go out for burgers and a movie. We'd all have a chance to visit together later.

Right on time, Mac's car pulled into the driveway. Randy went out to meet his friend while I stayed inside to finish making their meal. I'd give them a minute. After setting the table, I poured two glasses of iced tea and pulled homemade rolls out of the oven. I'd assumed the guys would be coming right on in, but so far they hadn't, and dinner was about ready. *What's taking them so long?* I wondered. As I rinsed out a pan, I glanced out the window over my kitchen sink. That's when I discovered the unexpected activity going on in my yard. I dried my hands and stepped outside for a closer look.

"Mac! Welcome!"

He was on his knees—

"Good to see you!"

—in my flowerbed—

"Glad you made it."

—digging up weeds.

"Mac?" I looked questioningly over our guest's head. Randy just grinned and shrugged his shoulders as if to say, *Don't look at me; I don't have a clue what he's doing either.*

Mac rose up. "I brought you a flat of pansies. Okay if I plant them right here?"

Just like that. Haven't seen the guy in forever, and before he sets a foot in my house, he's planting flowers in my yard.

"They'll last all winter. Just need a little sun and water. Some Miracle-Gro wouldn't hurt. Got any?"

I didn't.

But after Mac went home I got some.

The stuff worked, and in the next couple of weeks, those pansies took off. Spread like crazy. They looked beautiful; my neighbors told me so.

Today I made a foolish, tiptoe-because-I-was-barefoot outside run to retrieve the morning newspaper from its spot on the frosty grass of our front yard. Scurrying back toward the warmth of the house, thinking only of a cup of strong coffee with cream, my eyes fell on the pansies Mac planted last fall—purple and yellow, strong and healthy. Hardy squatters among a bed full of dead-from-the-cold stuff, they showed themselves to be crazily alive and well—exuberant with cheer and color.

Much like the guy who planted them.

I'm still not sure what possessed Mac to play gardener for me that day. I'm glad he did though, because every time I look at those flowers, I'm reminded of his unexpected act of kindness—an act that brings pleasure to me still.

And isn't that the power of kindness—that it lives on in the memory? Most all of us can recall times when we experienced love that was expressed in thoughtful, unexpected deeds. So often, in the dead-from-the-cold times of our lives, it's the small acts—the flowers someone plants when we aren't even looking—that touch us the most.

So although it's important that our daughters learn valuable skills like how to make friends, manage their money, obtain good grades, and be healthy and fit and strong, let's make sure we find time to teach them about kindness. In the garden, I believe, is a good place to start:

Mac's "Miracle-Grow" Gardening Tips

1. Get down on your knees.
2. Don't be afraid to get dirty.
3. Pull up some weeds.
4. Plant flowers that will last through the winter.

HOME AGAIN

Like everything else, teaching kindness starts at home. Displaying good manners—something as simple as always saying "please" and "thank you"—and insisting that family members treat each other with dignity and respect lays the foundation for the way our daughters will treat those who are outside the family.

Doing helpful, unasked-for good deeds—easy things like rolling up Dad's car windows when it starts to rain, saving the last piece of cake for a brother, taking a sister's popcorn bowl to the kitchen as you go—set a model of kindness. Family members can and should be taught, by example and by instruction, to do simple compassionate tasks for each other. They should be praised and acknowledged when they do, nudged into action when they don't.

Empathizing and offering comfort when a family member has a problem—a failed test grade, a lost friendship, an illness, or a fender bender in the car—teaches a big lesson. No one has to "go it alone." We're all in this together, and we need each other to make it through.

Others First

Nothing warms our hearts more than "feel-good" stories—ones we've seen on the evening news or read in the local paper. We love hearing about people who have sacrificed their time, their money, perhaps even their lives, to make things better for others. How wonderful it is when we learn of some kind deed our own daughter has done, either from her telling us about it or, better yet, by hearing of it from someone else.

It's right that our hearts be warmed. One way we show our love for the Father is by treating His kids—those around us—with caring, compassionate kindness. Developing and encouraging attitudes of kindness in our daughters begins with teaching them, at this most self-centered of ages, to think of someone other than themselves. Since attitude often follows action, exposing a girl to situations where it's easy for her to do good deeds for others is a great place to start.

Girl Scouts, Christian service clubs, and some school and church youth groups provide opportunities for a girl to do nice things for someone else. Participating in a group project such as gleaning a vegetable garden for a local food bank, visiting residents at a nursing home, or painting an elderly person's porch makes volunteering enjoyable for girls. Having fun while she's doing something worthwhile with her friends is the ultimate in positive peer pressure for your daughter. Encourage it!

Show Her How It's Done

Moms and daughters can perform compassionate deeds together. While you're preparing a casserole to take to a family in crisis, ask her to make a salad or dessert. Deliver the meal together. Keep the visit short, but take her along when you go to call on someone in town who's newly widowed. In the drugstore, while you shop for other items, she can pick out a sympathy card to send to a bereaved family at church. Be sure to purchase the one she chooses. When donations are needed for a family whose house has burned, show her the clothing you're giving from your own closet. Explain to her why you picked specific items to donate: The mom will need a warm sweater since the weather has turned cool. All women need at least one nice dress. A pink blouse always looks good. Ask that she thoughtfully select things from her closet too.

We know that kindness is more than good deeds. It's about a sensitivity of the heart—a tenderness we seek to develop in our girls. We can teach them by our words and our attitudes to look at others through the eyes of forgiveness and love.

Some of us are by nature tolerant and easygoing. What a blessing! Unfortunately, many of us fight an inborn tendency to be impatient and critical. It's important that we share with our daughters the times when we fail in our quest to be kind. Our girls need to see us apologize when we've been rude to a sales clerk or snappy with a family member. They need to hear the words "I'm sorry" when we've been unkind to them.

Doing More

I hold in the highest esteem those loving couples and families who provide long-term care for foster children. Our family did it for only a few short years, and I readily confess that though foster parenting was both rewarding and fulfilling, those years were among the most difficult ones in our family's history. The experience was stressful, sometimes discouraging, always exhausting, and relentlessly heartbreaking.

But oh, what we gained from it all! The children and their broken families changed us forever—especially Rachel. It was during those years that she learned about baby shots and diaper rash and the troubles other people face. It was then that she learned to buckle a toddler into a car seat and to sleep with the light on and to share everything that she had. And it was then—at that young, young age—that she developed a rare depth of compassion and tenderness.

Short-term medical mission trips to third-world countries, most often to rural Mexico, have been part of our family's summer plans for more than a decade. We, along with other like-minded Christian team members, spend about a week a year providing free medical care to some of the poorest people on earth. We love doing it. Serving in this way has provided us with rich cultural experiences. We've seen amazing sights and made friends with wonderful people from all over the world.

All of us, including Rachel, have been moved to greater depths of compassion and kindness by the sights we've seen, the people we've served. We return from each and every trip renewed in our hearts, ablaze in our spirits, ready to lay down our lives for each other a bit more each day.

Both of these experiences—foster parenting and serving on mission trips—have impacted Rachel in lasting ways. I realize that neither of these choices are made by the mainstream. Not many families go on mission trips, and few families take in foster children. Neither choice would be possible for most people. So are we special? Unique in some way? Different from other folks? Nope. We're not. Not in any way. What we've done is of no greater or lesser value than any other acts of service. All we've done is taken God up on the opportunities He's placed before us. We made the calls, answered the ad, signed ourselves up.

Individuals and families are continually called to greater depths of compassion and kindness. I'm convinced that we are frequently presented by the Father with unique opportunities to take a baby step or two out of our comfort zones and into greater areas of service. He places people and situations in our path who need *our* demonstrations of kindness.

What do we choose to do with those opportunities? How do we answer His call? Does this sound scary? It's not. God doesn't give us jobs that He doesn't equip us for. Rarely does He give us a task to do that we're going to hate. There are no really *important* jobs, and none so *unimportant* that they can go undone. There's just work to do, service to be offered, kindness to be shown.

Think about it. What is God calling you and your daughter to do? Today? This weekend? This summer? This year? What's your answer going to be?

Got your gardening gloves on? You may need them!

Trashy Neighbors

Within a day and a half of moving into our new house in our new town—a small community where we still knew no one—Randy and I received one of those unexpected, unplanned-for late-evening phone calls. A distant relative had passed away in a town located on the other side of the state. Plans were being made for what we in the south call "visitation," as well as for the funeral. Extended family members from near and far were expected to gather. What about us? It was a long way to travel, and we'd just moved and all, but *could we come?* Would Randy be a pallbearer?

Of course we could and of course he would. Unpacking would have to wait while we made the necessary arrangements for the unexpected trip. I stayed up past midnight getting things done. First I located and packed clothes for the kids and me. Then I starched and ironed Randy a long-sleeved white shirt. Finally I baked a fancy cream-cheese pound cake. (No self-respecting woman in my family would *ever* travel to a funeral—even one clear across the state—without a cake or a pie or a plate of brownies on her knees.)

Early the next morning, Randy called his boss to let him know he'd be gone a few days, poured out extra food and water for the cat, and sorted, stamped, and sealed the bills that would come due before we returned.

At the last minute—the kids and I had already gotten into the car and buckled up—Randy remembered one last important task. The three of us watched as he hauled four aromatic, bulging, black plastic sacks from the garage to the curb. Today was Wednesday. Our rural once-a-week garbage pickup wasn't scheduled until Friday, but that was just too bad. Unsightly as it was sitting there, Randy had no choice. The stinking stuff *had* to go out.

While we waited in the hot car, he dashed back inside to wash his hands. Finally, we backed from the driveway.

It was more than a week after our return to town when—while shopping at the five-and-dime for paper towels and a dish drainer (no automatic dishwasher in our new house)—I accidentally learned of an unfortunate incident that had taken place in our absence.

"Your husband the new coach?" asked the friendly clerk.

"Yes ma'am. He is." I smiled.

"Y'all living in Miz Berry's old house?"

"We are. Moved in last Monday."

"Y'all sure 'nuff had a mess in your yard last week."

"Excuse me?"

"Them dogs." She shook her head sympathetically. "That pack of strays'll get in your trash ever time. You'll learn you cain't hardly put it out 'fore you see the truck coming. It must have took you and your husband half a day to get that mess cleaned up."

Mess? What mess? When we had returned from the funeral, it was to a house and yard that looked the same as when we'd left. There had been no trash anywhere. "You must be mistaken. Maybe it was another house."

"Third on the right? Hickory Ridge Road?"

That was the one.

By then we'd met all our neighbors. (Granted, there weren't that many. Only seven houses sit on the dead-end street.) But one house at a time, they had all come calling on the day we'd returned from the funeral. "Sorry to hear about your loss." "Anything we can do?" The women had brought us casseroles and cornbread and cut flowers from their beds, had helpfully told me where I could get my hair cut and who in town babysat.

Their husbands had shaken Randy's hand, spouted good-natured advice, and made uninformed predictions about this year's football team. (Never mind that Randy's sport is girls' basketball. *He's a coach, isn't he?*)

One by one, they welcomed us to the neighborhood and invited us to come visit their churches—Wesley Methodist, First Baptist, Harmony Assembly of God. We'd be welcome at any of them. Hoped to see us come Sunday.

Standing outside the five-and-dime, absorbing the clerk's puzzling words, I realized that in all that visiting, with all those introductions, and during all those words of small talk, not one neighbor had said a word about trash. They'd had plenty of chances all right, but I couldn't recall a single comment about what it had been like to go out and pick up the smelly, strewn-around garbage of some just-moved-in-from-out-of-town family—folks who might just be one brick short of a load, seeing as how they were ignorant enough to put their trash out *two days early.*

Not a word.

And you know, it's been six years since we moved to the neighborhood, and we still don't know who it was who cleaned up our garbage for us. They won't say. However, now that we've lived here awhile I guess I understand why.

To confess to a good deed, folks around here say, *is to give up your blessin'.*

Why would a person ever want to do that?

Have to be crazy.

I guess you would.

Do not let your left hand know what your right hand is doing,
so that your giving may be in secret.
Then your Father, who sees what is done in secret,
will reward you.

—MATTHEW 6:3,4

Putting It into Practice

1. Adopt an elderly neighbor or a resident in a local nursing home. Ask your daughter who it should be. Remember your adoptee on her birthday and on other holidays. Visit her regularly. Send her cards. Take her homemade treats and flowers from your yard.

2. Be sneaky. With your daughter, prepare small loaves of banana bread. Wrap them up and attach little notes that say "Somebody loves you!" On a Saturday morning, gently place the loaves on the doorsteps of nearby neighbors. Ring the bell and run!

3. Invite a little girl over for the afternoon. Encourage your daughter to spend special time with her. Join in yourself. Color pictures, paint fingernails, braid hair, and have a snack.

4. Write letters to a missionary family. Provide your daughter with cute stationery so she can write to the children. Encourage her to send frequent notes, cards, cartoons, and jokes. Pray together for your faraway friends.

13

This Little Light of Mine

A Ticklish Pause

One sunny Sunday morning shortly after their third birthday, my four-years-younger-than-me twin brothers concluded, right during the middle of church, that they needed to go to the bathroom.

Couldn't wait.

From the very beginning they have been masters at tag-teaming our parents. So even though their desperate need to go coincided suspiciously with the beginning of the preacher's long, sit-there-and-be-still-I'm-not-going-to-tell-you-two-again sermon, what's a parent to do when faced with a pair of weak-bladdered boys who hours earlier, it is suddenly remembered, *did* gulp down a full half-gallon jug of breakfast juice?

That parent is beat before he starts. He knows it.

Faced with these stacked odds, my dad did what had to be done. Leaving my mother and me behind, he slipped from the pew, guided the boys out, and quickly followed them up the aisle to the back foyer, where the restrooms were located.

The preacher of the 400-member church we attended was a well-trained young man who believed in the Power Of The Pause. His speaking style included frequent insertions of moments of silence—fully 60 seconds long—designed to let his last-spoken point sink in. Careful about such things, he saw to it that each Sunday sermon included at least four of these strategically placed periods of quiet. The good man meant well. Unfortunately he was blissfully unaware that the cumulative effect of all of those verbal starts and stops was that his words tended not to flow meaningfully along, but to fly at his patient parishioners in distracting, difficult-to-follow spits and spurts.

Blessedly for him, the congregation—his very first—was possessed of a pleasant nature. To their credit, the good members confined their opinions to their cars when headed home and tried their meager best, week after week, to follow along.

It was right in the middle of a rather unfortunately timed pause that my dad returned, post-bathroom, with my two brothers. Business taken care of, he firmly nudged them into what would shortly prove itself to be a poorly chosen near-the-front pew. Rather than scooting toward the middle, they—as kids are prone to do—plopped right down on the end of the bench. Four little legs stuck straight out, blocking my dad's entrance, leaving him—except for the (at the moment) mute preacher—the only man in the building standing. It was impossible for him to sit down until the boys moved over.

"Scoot down. Now. Both of you," he hissed between clenched teeth.

They weren't moving.

In fact, in their haste to share some important information they had forgotten all about Daddy. Neither of them were paying him a bit of attention. There was a bathroom report to be given—"Mommy! Mommy!" in high-pitched, loud-enough-for-the-whole-church-to-hear unison, "Dad potty too! Dad potty too!"

He doesn't remember *how* he got them out of the way. He may even have sat *on top of* one of the boys. All my dad knows is that amid a chorus of snickers, chuckles, and outright guffaws, he managed to find a place to sit. Fast.

The twins' mid-service announcement provided funny fodder for lots of Sunday dinners that day. "Did you see Louie's red face?"—of my dad. "And what about poor Preacher!" Knees were slapped and iced tea snorted. "Those boys!"

By some weeks after the incident, most was forgotten. However, compassionate congregants did wonder if the commotion had shaken the preacher up more than was realized. For as far as anyone can remember, that Sunday marked the end of the Power Of The Pause.

More to It

When my children were small, I was sure that if only I could manage to rear them to the age where they would sit still and remain quiet during church—to the time when they would finally make it through a whole hour service without a trip to the potty—the remainder of my job as spiritual teacher would be comparatively easy. Teaching them to pray and love Jesus would surely be a breeze compared to the rising panic I felt on the Sundays when my stash of Cheerios threatened to run out before the last "amen" was spoken.

Right.

"Why do some people get well when we pray and some people don't?"

"How come only men preach at our church?"

"How do we know God really wrote the Bible?"

How and why indeed? Little did I realize that I'd be expected to answer these and a gazillion other questions as my daughter grew out of toddlerhood and into adolescence.

"Okay God, You're gonna have to help me on this one," became my daily plea. I find I'm not alone. These are challenging

years, years when believe-anything-you-tell-them little girls grow into questioning, discerning, sometimes doubting young women. Almost every mother of faith I know claims some version of my heartfelt prayer as her own. Over and over we find ourselves at a loss as to what to say, the best way to guide, how to answer. And so down on our knees we fall, begging and imploring Him to help us raise these girls of ours—correction, these girls of *His*—to love and know Him as their Father and Friend.

Thankfully, He does.

Home Is Where It's At

When our family moved from a good-sized town with a wonderful, active church youth group to a tiny community where none of the local churches offered much in the way of teen opportunities, we began to wonder about our children's spiritual health. It was Kent, the youth leader from the church we were leaving, who corrected the assumptions I'd started to make.

"Annette," he explained, "folks have done a bunch of research about what turns faithful kids into faithful adults. The results aren't what you'd expect. It's not so much whether or not a kid is active in a church youth group that predicts the outcome as it is the home where he or she grows up. Parents are what makes the difference. Your kids will be fine."

And so far they are. Though I wish they'd had the opportunities to grow up as I did, in a big church where the youth group would have been a central part of both their spiritual and social lives, they have managed to develop a strong faith, a personal relationship with God the Father, and to live moral, mostly obedient lives so far. Our family has recently begun worshiping with a larger church in a neighboring town, where there are a bunch of teens for Rachel to hang out with. She's loving it, and I'm happy for her, but nothing has changed as far as who's responsible for her spiritual growth and development. We, her parents, are!

She's Always Watching

My friend Kent intended to make me feel better by telling me that it was *I* who would determine the quality of my daughter's spiritual life, not the church youth program. *Oh no,* I thought, *I have no one to blame things on but myself.* His words offered not comfort, but conviction! It's true. Because instead of being a consistent example of the faithful Christian woman I want Rachel to grow up to be, I mess up with discouraging, disgusting regularity.

What adolescents *cannot* tolerate are adults who claim to be perfect, then prove not to be. Since none of us will *ever* get it right, since not one of us can manage a sinless life, I suggest employing a different strategy. First off, we moms must dedicate ourselves to doing our personal best to love, honor, and obey God with our every thought, word, and deed.

That, in some ways, is the easy part.

But just as important, yet often more difficult, is being willing to admit that we fall short. We need to selectively share some of the spiritual struggles we face—gossip, misplaced priorities, disrespect toward a coworker, pride, laziness (to confess a few of my own). Doing so teaches our girls that struggles aren't the problem. Everyone, including Mom, has them. The problem is that all of us want to ignore our failings. It's our nature—and it's easier that way, we think. But that's not God's plan. We—both moms and daughters—are to lay our weaknesses at the feet of Jesus, recognizing and acknowledging that it's because of the love of the Father that we get to start over, again and again. In this, we moms must try our very hardest to live as righteous examples before our girls.

This lesson, if we teach it well, can sustain our daughter should she at some point in her life find herself in *really big trouble.* We all sin, sometimes intentionally and willfully; other times, occasionally—almost accidentally. Too often, imperfect teens and young adults mistakenly feel that what they've done is so bad, so unforgivable, that God wants nothing to do with them. They feel so unacceptable before Him that, rather than face the pain of their guilt, they turn away from God completely. Sometimes they don't turn back.

I have spoken with many, many adult women whose relationships with God are marked by coldness and distance—most often because of the guilt they feel over something done in their youth. They were never taught how to accept His grace and start over.

A daughter needs to see her mom model confession, repentance, and forgiveness. Speak of spiritual things at home. Post Scriptures on the fridge. Tell her why a particular verse is there. Share little gleanings from your personal Bible study time with her. Talk to her about what you learned in Sunday school. Ask her to pray for one of your friends. Encourage her to speak of her own concerns, but don't press. If spiritual conversation flows naturally from your heart and your lips, it will, in time, flow from hers as well.

It Takes a Church to Raise a Child

A loving church family is invaluable to a growing girl. From her Sunday-school teacher she learns about Bible characters and events—the foundations of her religion. From her youth leader she learns about faith and focus on Jesus. From pastors and preachers she learns about virtue, sin, and redemption.

And from the individual members who take an interest in her, she learns about care, concern, and accountability.

Active membership in a church body is of great importance in the raising of a healthy, spiritually grounded young woman. A supportive body of believers helps her to understand that individual Christians don't stand alone but are a part of something much bigger. It gives her a place to feel she belongs.

Moms who place active involvement in a local church high on their list of priorities demonstrate the value of love and service to their daughters. Church shouldn't be simply a place where we go, but a body to which we belong. Our family's involvement should be such that if we moved away or stopped coming, others would have to take over our areas of service. Our presence should make a difference.

Our daughters need to be active in the areas of work, worship, and fellowship. They will benefit from exposure to all members of the body, not just other teens. Much can be learned when they work in the church nursery alongside an older woman, help a young mother teach the four-year-olds, or assist the minister's middle-aged wife shelve books in the church library. Look for such opportunities.

A good church for our teens is one that respectfully considers them to be valuable members of *today's* church, *not* one that waits for them to be the church of the *future.*

It's Okay to Question

In today's multicultural climate, our girls will be exposed over and over again to various non-Christian world religions, as well as to a multitude of faddish New Age beliefs. Even if they have been thoroughly grounded in the Christian faith, girls may express a fascination with some of these traditions. How should a mom respond to such an interest?

By learning all she can. If a daughter is enamored with Buddhism, Mom should read up on it. If a girl comes home speaking about reincarnation, Mom needs to know what she's talking about. Only when we know of what we speak can we counter the options our daughters are facing with the reality of the gospel of Christ.

There is nothing wrong with a daughter's asking questions. We'd just better have some answers. If we find ourselves in over our heads (and some waters *do* run deep), if our daughter appears to have more than a passing interest in an alternative religion, it's time to seek professional spiritual guidance. Ministers, counselors, or educated Bible teachers should be consulted. Inviting such a person into our home to visit with our daughter and to answer her questions can provide a nonthreatening way to deal with a serious issue.

When our daughters leave our homes, we will no longer have the opportunity to control where they will go to church, how often they will attend, or even if they will go at all. But at this age we can and should. Just as we see to it that they go to school, visit the doctor and the dentist regularly, and eat properly and get enough rest, we are responsible to see to their spiritual habits. Adolescent girls are not ready to be given the choice whether or not—or even where—to go to church. We, as their parents, have the responsibility to prayerfully, thoughtfully, and with as much information as possible choose the right church for ourselves and our daughters.

Start with Prayer

When we mothers start to truly understand the magnitude of our responsibility to turn our daughters' hearts toward the Father, we can easily become overwhelmed. There is no way we can do it alone. How great is the news that we don't have to! God hasn't given us an impossible task, but has simply presented us with one that's impossible to do without His help.

Each of us is different. Some mothers pray in a steady stream of words, talking to God conversationally all day long. Others prefer the more organized approach of a set time every day. But both ways serve to address our concerns and requests to the Father, the One who loves, listens, and responds. *There is nothing we can do for our daughters that is more important than praying for them.*

Few spoken words have the power to convey love, tenderness, and concern like the phrase "I'm praying for you." Make these words part of daily conversation. If you're not accustomed to telling your daughter you are praying for her, repetition will help the words to flow as naturally from your lips as "I washed your soccer uniform" or "Dinner's almost ready" or "Wear a jacket—it's supposed to turn cold."

Your daughter needs to hear you say the words.

THE PRAYER

Brandy was going to Bosnia. There was no turning back, for she had received her deployment papers. Everyone knows orders are orders. That's how the United States military operates. It was a fact understood by all.

All, that is, except for one adoring, admiring, nine-year-old little girl.

Rachel and Brandy became fast friends during the year Brandy respectfully called Rachel's daddy "Coach." An 18-year-old senior, long-legged and strong, she played on Randy's high-school basketball team, the mighty Lady Indians. (Granted, the school's choice of mascots might sound a bit racist to some. *No offense intended*, the administrators kindly assure everyone. Political correctness, it seems, has been a bit slow to reach our tiny forest town.)

The Lady Indians were pretty good that year. Thanks in part to Brandy's skill, they won games both away and at home. Brandy was the kind of player, Randy told me, that a coach wishes he had a whole team of. Were he to note the best players he's coached during his almost 20-year career, no doubt Brandy would make the short list. She consistently displayed her athletic talents, made full use of her skill and stamina each time she hit the court. However, it was her attitude and behavior off the court that made Brandy so special. Well respected by teachers and students alike, she was a bubbly, vivacious leader—poised, popular, and very pretty.

None of those qualities were what made the coach's daughter love her so. It was the gentle, undivided attention that Brandy showered on her that so endeared the older girl to Rachel's heart. Every afternoon, when school was let out, Rachel would run at top speed—from the elementary building—down the sidewalk—across the playground—into the high school gym where Randy would be hurriedly preparing for after-school practice. Monday through Friday, unless a game was scheduled, Rachel would arrive to find Brandy waiting for her. She'd be sitting midway up the bleachers, dressed and ready for practice with a few minutes to spare. A huge smile would spread over Rachel's face, and she would race up the steps to give Brandy a big out-of-breath hug before settling in for a hasty girl-to-girl chat.

It didn't seem to matter that the difference in their ages spanned almost a decade. You'd have thought the two of them were best friends. I'm not sure they weren't. Each afternoon, Rachel would show Brandy what she'd done in school. Almost every day, Brandy would smooth and brush

Rachel's long, tangled hair. Sometimes Brandy bought Rachel a Coke. Often they shared a candy bar.

The two exchanged birthday cards and inexpensive Christmas presents, and occasionally, if she happened to be driving out our way, Brandy stopped by, picked Rachel up, and took her into town where she treated her to a Dairy Queen shake and french fries.

Not much is as endearing to a parent as someone who makes her child feel special. I was no exception. I loved Brandy because she loved Rachel. It was as simple as that.

On one early spring day Rachel learned that Brandy, soon to graduate, had joined the army—and when it was explained to her what exactly that meant, she cried and asked why her friend was going.

There were lots of reasons. Just ask her recruiter. (Small towns like ours, which graduate crop after crop of bright, hard-working, economically disadvantaged students, provide fertile fields just ripe for military picking. Show a well-made recruitment film to a kid who's been out of his home state only twice in his life and you're bound to inspire a surge of pimple-faced patriotism. It's no wonder the recruiters hang around the campus and make calls during supper.) She could see the world, learn a skill, go to college—worthy goals, all of them. The several military offers Brandy received were certainly worth serious consideration. For as good a player as she was, when her dreams of a college basketball scholarship failed to come to pass—not quite tall enough, a little too slow—it seemed unlikely that her dreams of a university education would come true either.

Brandy's working-class parents loved her dearly, wanted good things for her, but neither of them had gone to college, and they'd not saved up for their daughter to go either. It would be tough, maybe impossible, for her to finance an education on her own. Joining the army would surely make things easier for everyone.

Surely.

So less than a month after receiving her high-school diploma, Brandy enlisted in the United States Army. She completed basic training, then was sent out of state for advanced schooling in something having to do with biological warfare. There she learned to work in a laboratory, performing her tasks garbed in an airtight, spacesuit-like garment. During this time she and Rachel kept in touch, writing letters back and forth. Rachel's mail was kept private, and I didn't pry, but from what I gathered from the little bit she shared with me, her friend was doing well. As it worked out, Brandy would get to come home at Christmas for a nice long visit. Rachel couldn't wait.

It was while visiting a neighboring community's high-school gymnasium that Randy and I first learned of Brandy's impending, unexpected, early overseas deployment. Her parents, there to cheer her younger sister's freshman basketball game, broke the news to a parking-lot circle of concerned hometown fans. We stood motionless on the gravel, squinting into the sun, listening as they explained. Since war had broken out in Bosnia, U.S. troops were getting ready to be sent out. Their Brandy, *our Brandy*, would be among the first to go.

Bosnia? None of us in that little group could recall exactly where the place was. Her parents, still in shock, couldn't tell us much either. Though they'd studied the location on a map, all they really knew was that Bosnia was halfway around the world and that it was pretty far north. Their oldest daughter, the one who'd never seen snow, was going to spend the winter in one of the coldest places on earth. She would leave before Christmas.

Suddenly, joining the army was about more than seeing the world and a free education. Cloudy faces betrayed silent thoughts. No longer did it seem that things would be easier after all.

During the drive home, Randy and I were silent for a long while. How would we break the news to Rachel? How should she be told? There was a *war* going on over there. What if Brandy didn't come back? It *could* happen.

How did Rachel take the news?

Not well. She simply wasn't going to have it. Brandy was *not* going to Bosnia. Her friend was coming home for Christmas. End of discussion.

I tried to explain, to reason with her. Her daddy tried too. "Rachel, when Brandy joined the army, she knew she might have to go far away. It's her job. She doesn't have a choice."

"Does she *want* to go?"

"No, but—"

"She's not going to have to then. I'm going to pray. Every night. I'll pray that Brandy doesn't have to go to Bosnia. God will make it so she doesn't have to go."

Randy and I looked at each other over her head. "Honey," I spoke firmly. "You can pray for God to take care of Brandy while she's gone. We all will. But it's too late to pray she won't have to go. She's already gotten her orders. They can't be changed."

"God can change them. I'm going to my room to pray right now." Primly she marched to her room and closed the door. There would be no more talk about it. She wouldn't have it. Nor did she care to contribute to the collection of cards and letters that folks from town were preparing to send ahead to Bosnia so Brandy would have mail from home when she arrived at that cold place. *No thanks.*

Ours is a religious community, a Christian town. We pride ourselves on trusting in the Lord to take care of things. He always does. We trusted Him this time to take care of our girl. As the day of Brandy's departure drew near, Randy and I, along with her mom and her dad, the faithful pastors of every church in town, and numerous friends and extended family members from across the state, prayed day and night for God to please keep watch over, protect, and guard our Brandy when she went to Bosnia. We prayed hard that He would help her to do a good job, and that when her time was up, He would *bring her home safe.*

Rachel, still not knowing any better, prayed that she wouldn't go at all.

And she didn't. *Brandy didn't go.*

Just like that, her orders were rescinded. Papers that had already been signed, sealed, and delivered were, at the last minute, voided. Precise military personnel plans were scrapped. Thrown out. Tabled. Changed.

So was my sorry, self-righteous, all-grown-up faith.

Rachel took the news that Brandy wouldn't be going rather casually. She didn't appear even a bit surprised. Acted as if she'd known it all along.

Perhaps she had.

And Jesus prayed this prayer:
"O Father, Lord of heaven and earth,
thank you for hiding the truth from those
who think themselves so wise,
and for revealing it to little children.
Yes, Father, for it pleased you to do it this way!"
—MATTHEW 11:25,26 (TLB)

Growing Together in Faith

1. With your daughter's input, select a month's worth of daily Bible verses for you and her to read independently. Once a week, meet to compare notes, to share what verses have been the most meaningful, to discuss passages that may have been difficult to understand.

2. Be sure your daughter has a Bible she can understand. Many easy-to-read student versions are available. Ask a minister for help in picking the one best for your daughter. Surprise her with a pretty cover for her Bible.

3. As a family, skip dinner one night a week. Do something fun, like playing a game, to distract each other from the hunger. Contribute the amount that would have been spent on the meal to a missionary or to a children's home.

4. Surround your daughter with inspirational sayings and Scriptures. Visit a Christian bookstore to find faith-affirming daily calendars, framed prints, note cards, and stationery.

A Few Last Words

I don't recall what the argument was about, but I'm sure it involved some matter of dire consequence to character like shoes left on the floor, blue nail polish on the kitchen counter, or a shirt worn unironed. Whatever started it, this was one of those mother-daughter conflicts that seemed to take on a life of its own. In record time, 12-year-old Rachel and I both accelerated past the point of reasonable return. Tempers flared. Voices were raised. Doors slammed.

Possessing an all-purpose ability to ignore such estrogen-powered dramatics, Randy, nestled snugly in his recliner, managed to finish reading the entire evening newspaper before coming to the uncomfortable realization that his daughter and his wife were both crying behind locked doors, and had in fact been wailing for at least half an hour.

Now you'd think that such an obviously intelligent person as my husband would go directly to his wayward daughter and straighten her out, wouldn't you? Me too. When, between sobs, I heard him knocking on the bathroom door, I assumed he had done just that. So I unlocked it.

Not so. I was *first* on Randy's list of stops. His face was close to mine, and he spoke in a not-too-friendly voice. "Rachel gets to you sometimes. She does to me too. But you've got to learn to deal with her better than this."

What? No sympathy? Not even a hug?

"Annette," he said evenly, "*one* of you has *got* to be the adult."

Ouch.

I relate this embarrassing story because at that very moment, I came to the tragic, repentant conclusion that I was the worst mother on the planet. I had, with my unreasonable behavior and nasty words, surely ruined my daughter for life. Perhaps, if she was lucky, years of therapy might salvage just a bit of her soul, but I was not going to hold out much hope.

I was ashamed, for it was just as I'd feared. I did not deserve to be *anyone's* mother. I certainly had no rightful claim to the 12 years' worth of Mother's Day cards stashed in the back of my underwear drawer, and never again could I wear my "World's Greatest Mom" sweatshirt.

Ever felt that way? Ever wanted, because of some awful parenting blunder, maybe even a *series* of terrible mistakes, to just crawl under the covers and never come out?

If so, dear sister, you're not alone. Many, many mothers have shared with me the ways in which, over and over, they blow it with their adolescent girls. They tell me about getting tired and cranky and making unreasonable demands. They confess to making mountains out of molehills and molehills out of mountains, and to sometimes picking at their beloved daughters until they make them cry.

My wish in writing this book has been to offer hope and encouragement to the mom who, like me, sometimes wonders whether she's getting any of this adolescent parenting right. To the mom who finds herself in shock and at a loss as to how to deal with this amazing creature—the one who used to be her little girl but suddenly isn't anymore—I've attempted to give some insight and suggestions and encouragement that can help her make it along.

My message to mothers is, be assured that you are doing so much so right. Perfection isn't expected. The seemingly huge problems that loom today will be forgotten tomorrow.

Girls thrive—both in spite of and because of us—if they know they are loved. Strive above all else to make sure your daughter *knows* that you love her. Show her, tell her, write it to her. Over and over. Again and again. Sometimes, like you, she doesn't feel very lovable or worthy, and it's easy for her to forget.

Treasure the good times.

Let go of the bad times.

Forgive her.

Forgive yourself.

Never get off your knees.

And may God bless you in your task.